The Essential
Vegan
Cookbook

ISABEL HOOD

Published in Great Britain in 2019 by
need2know
Remus House
Coltsfoot Drive
Peterborough
PE2 9BF
Telephone 01733 898103
www.need2knowbooks.co.uk

All Rights Reserved
© Isabel Hood
SB ISBN 978-1-91084-388-8
Cover photograph: Adobe Stock

Contents

Chapter 4: Pulses and Grains – Comfort and Joy 51

Chapter 5: Nuts, Seeds and Oils – Opulence and Intensity 85

Chapter 6: Fresh Herbs – Aroma and Fragrance 113

Chapter 7: Chilli and Spice – Warmth and Seasoning 147

Introduction

Ever since I was a child, the kitchen has been my favourite room in the house – it is a rich, aromatic, comforting space where magic and alchemy take place, where different, often disparate, ingredients are combined and somehow come together into a delectable, nourishing whole. Food and my kitchen make up the engine which drives my life, and as far back as I can remember, cooking and eating have been at the very centre of my existence. I was lucky enough to be brought up in Mexico and fed by Mexican cooks throughout my childhood and formative years; I was also lucky enough to be educated at an international school with students from the four corners of the Earth, and meals at friends' houses were a real adventure which introduced me to countless other gastronomic cultures. A career in food was the natural and predictable result and throughout my adult life I have immersed myself in the cuisines of the world and delved into their origins and traditional or indigenous ingredients, including their extensive vegetarian and vegan cookery and abundance of sparkling, imaginative plant-based dishes.

As my interest in food has developed over the years, so has my fascination with the role it plays in human health and wellbeing. This has led me to research which foods and methods of cooking can best support me in my quest for energy and vitality, and for a long, healthy and happy life; and to try out and test different ways of eating, such as veganism and vegetarianism, macrobiotics, low-high fat and low-high protein, food combining, high-raw nutrition. The information and insight which I have acquired from these experiments, together with my knowledge of ethnic cuisines, have resulted in the development of a two-pronged personal approach to cooking: food which brings joy and pleasure, and also nourishes and supports health – and this can be a real challenge in the Western world of the 21st century!

We are bombarded on a daily basis with conflicting advice about the foods we should or should not eat, and attempting to follow this overload of guidance is exhausting, confusing, frustrating and enough to make any food lover's life an absolute misery of indecision and denial, as well as subjecting us to nutritional dictatorship and gastronomic renunciation.

One fact, however, invariably stands out: the health benefits of fresh fruit and vegetables. My intuition and plain logic have ever whispered to me that a 'natural' diet is the key to health and happiness, and throughout my long cooking career I seem to have travelled steadily along a road which has led me to the area of my life I call my 'Vegan Vie'. Plant-based food has never ceased to inspire and motivate me with its visions of open air markets, sun-drenched and exuberant; mountains of fruit and vegetables, bursting with life and colour and arranged with instinctive flair and artistry; straw baskets overflowing with sultry, aromatic spices; bunches of fragrant herbs, still damp from the morning dew; crates full to the brim with earthy nuts, seeds, pulses and grains – the pictures alone are enough to send me straight to my favourite room in the house, where I can begin to create magic with the infinity of ingredients from the world's vegan larder. I hope you enjoy the recipes from my Vegan Vie!

1

A Vegan Diet for the 21st Century

The term 'vegan' was coined by Donald Watson, a Yorkshire wood-worker and teacher, when he founded the Vegan Society in 1944. Born into a family of hearty, meat-eating trenchermen, he witnessed the slaughter of a pig on his uncle's farm in his teens and made a New Year's resolution never to eat an animal again – and when he died in 2005 at the age of 95, he had not touched meat or fish for 81 years. In the early 1900s, the word 'vegetarianism' described a diet which excluded all animal products but in the mid-1940s, when Watson found that this concept was broadening to include eggs and dairy products, he combined the first three and last two letters of 'vegetarian' – 'the beginning and end of vegetarianism' – to create the expression 'vegan'.

Donald Watson's culinary legacy is a diet centred wholly on plant-based foods. The Vegan Society describes veganism as 'a philosophy and way of living which seeks to exclude – as far as is possible and practical – all forms of exploitation of, and cruelty to, animals for food, clothing or any other purpose; and by extension, promotes the development and use of animal-free alternatives for the benefit of humans, animals and the environment. In dietary terms it denotes the practice of dispensing with all products derived wholly or partly from animals.'

If this description makes your heart sink and brings to mind visions of brown rice, brown lentils and even browner nut roasts, think again. A vegan diet is certainly based on fruit and vegetables, pulses and grains, nuts and seeds – but it also includes pungent herbs, warm aromatic spices, rich and fragrant oils, wickedly dark chocolate – and that is just a start. The plant world is infinitely varied and can provide a diet of utter pleasure in an endless spectrum of flavours, textures, scents and colours: crisp and crunchy, soft and tender, juicy or dense, sharp, sweet, spicy, light, heavy, strong, delicate, intense.

Look again at the nut roast, with its golden toasted walnuts, brazils and cashews, partnered not by a brown gravy made with Marmite, but a vibrant plum and cranberry chutney, or a Salsa Verde, sharp with green olives and capers and bright with fresh parsley, mint or basil. The brown rice may perhaps be cooked with a thick purée of tomatoes and smoky chillies, Mexican style, or stirred into a laksa, a satisfying Indonesian soup redolent with coconut and lemon grass; and the lentils might be slate green rather than brown, combined with silky roasted peppers, coriander, pickled lemons, pine nuts and raisins to create a lively, earthy Middle Eastern salad. Now be honest – does any of this sound in the least bit dreary, let alone 'brown'?

So often when I mention the word 'vegan', I instantly come up against a reinforced concrete wall of resistance. The reaction is invariably 'I could never give up meat, or fish or cheese or eggs.' But veganism is not about deprivation, or denying oneself the pleasure of food. The glass is not empty. On the contrary, it is full – full to the brim, full to overflowing. It contains a wealth of possibilities, which perhaps only a cook who has experimented extensively with vegetable cookery can truly understand. The diet of anybody who eats animal protein, including vegetarians, tends to be centred on these particular foods, with vegetables as the side dish, as a complement to the meat or the fish or the omelette. But a vegan cook's focus on vegetables has, out of necessity, to be infinitely broader, both in a search for adequate protein and a search for variety – vegetables, pulses and grains are undoubtedly satisfying and nutritious, but they can become very dull indeed in the hands of a lazy or unadventurous cook.

Plant-based cookery is limited only by our imaginations, and in the 21st century, we are blessed with almost year round availability of virtually every fruit and vegetable grown worldwide. While we need to be aware and conscious of the high environmental cost, we have at our disposal a boundless range of fresh food with which to nourish our bodies, and of ingredients with which to cook and create delicious, wholesome, healthy meals. The cuisines of every culture and nation are accessible to us nowadays through their indigenous fruits and vegetables and offer us countless opportunities and ideas. While the choice of animal products is wide but limited, it is surely impossible to ever tire of the plant kingdom and its immense diversity which is just waiting to be discovered, experimented and played around with, and combined in so many different ways.

This extraordinary wealth of fresh plant foods is extended even further by the range of other ingredients available to us: sharp fruity vinegars, richly flavoured extra virgin oils – from pumpkin seed to avocado, fresh herbs, seed and nut butters, condiments like tamari and shoyu, pickled lemons, seaweeds (a fabulous source of natural minerals!), mustards, sun-dried tomatoes, olives, capers, fresh, smoked and dried chillies, spices, miso, tamarind, sumac berries, dried wild mushrooms, pomegranate molasses, Sichuan peppercorns, wasabi paste – the list is endless and astonishingly versatile, providing countless possibilities and opportunities for delicious, healthy, natural dishes.

'Plant-based cookery is limited only by our imaginations.'

And if the promise of sheer pleasure from this infinite gastronomic palette of colours, textures and flavour sensations is not enough to entice you into the magical world of plant cookery, think of the benefits:

- While we are constantly being exhorted to eat our 'five-a-day', many people admit that they find this difficult. By simply incorporating more vegan dishes into your everyday life, 'five-a-day' turns into '20-a-day' without thought, let alone effort, and provides all those essential vitamins, minerals, antioxidants, enzymes and phytonutrients.

- Among the 21st century's greatest challenges, global warming and environmental pollution must surely play centre stage. A vegan diet offers a sustainable way of eating and living, with infinitely less planetary impact than a diet based on animal protein, let alone convenience foods. Every single food choice we make affects the world in which we live, for better or for worse, and veganism undoubtedly scores on the 'better' side.

- With so many horror stories about animal welfare hitting the headlines on a regular basis, a plant-based diet becomes ever more attractive and coherent.

- The cost of food has been spiralling over the last few years, and a vegan diet, with its emphasis on fruit and vegetables, grains, pulses and nuts, is considerably more economical than one based on meat and fish.

- And while we are on the subject of meat and fish, let's talk about protein and its many vegan sources. Grains and pulses, seeds and nuts, soya products, sea vegetables and fresh sprouts are all rich in protein; some, however, do not contain all 8 amino acids and it is therefore wise to combine them in order to create a 'complete' protein – black beans and corn, and chickpeas and couscous for instance.

Summing Up

A vegan diet is:

- Plant-based and excludes all animal products.
- Bursting with flavour, texture, colour and satisfaction, let alone nutritional potential and has nothing to do with 'boring', 'brown' or 'inadequate'.
- Centred around a virtually infinite spectrum of ingredients, drawn from the world larder.
- Environmentally friendly.
- Compassionate.
- Easy on the pocket.

2

The Vegan Kitchen

The vegan store cupboard

While the star ingredients in vegan cookery are fresh fruit and vegetables, a well-stocked store cupboard is essential. The following are some of the ingredients which you will find invaluable:

- Bouillon powder: a savoury, golden powder which can be used to make stock or as a seasoning and flavouring. Marigold Organic Swiss Vegetable Bouillon Powder is excellent and available in supermarkets.

- Organic vegetable stock cubes.

- Tinned tomatoes, beans (red kidney/black/butter/cannellini), chickpeas, sweetcorn.

- Dried fruit: raisins or sultanas, cranberries, apricots.

- Tamari and/or shoyu soy sauces.

- Wholemeal spaghetti, penne and pasta shells.

- Oriental noodles like soba and udon.

- Dried beans, lentils and chickpeas.

- Oils like olive, hazelnut, toasted sesame, truffle.

- Vinegars: red wine, cider, balsamic, rice wine.

- Spices: cumin, coriander, cardamom, fennel, black pepper, star anise, cinnamon, cloves, dried chillies, juniper berries, allspice berries.

- Agave nectar and/or runny honey.

- Sea salt.

- Sun-dried tomatoes and sun-dried tomato purée.

- Dried wild mushrooms.

- Green and black olives.

- Capers.

- Smooth and wholegrain mustard.

- Nuts: whole, flaked and ground almonds; whole, toasted and chopped hazelnuts; raw cashews, brazils, pine nuts, walnuts, pecans; roasted cashews and peanuts.

- Peanut butter and tahini.

- Cooking wine and cider.

'Most large supermarkets now stock almost everything you will need for your vegan culinary creations, including organic versions.'

Resources

- Most large supermarkets now stock almost everything you will need for your vegan culinary creations, including organic versions.

- Health shops are another good option, as are delicatessens.

- Farmers' markets are worth a visit, as the produce is usually very fresh and often much cheaper.

- Countless mail order firms can supply the slightly harder to find ingredients and some offer items like nuts and pulses in larger, better priced quantities.

The following are the ones I use on a regular basis:

- Seasoned Pioneers offer a bewildering selection of whole and ground spices, spice mixes, pastes and rubs, dried herbs, dried chillies and seasonings, including organic, from all over the world. Their prices and delivery charges are very reasonable, and my orders usually arrive within 48 hours. **www.seasonedpioneers.co.uk**

- Ethical Superstore stock a huge range of ingredients suitable for the vegan cook, including organic: oils, vinegars, mustards, tamari and shoyu, macrobiotic specialities, pulses and grains, nuts, dried fruit, seaweeds, spices, seasonings, curry pastes, etc, as well as household cleaning products and toiletries. Items can be ordered in bulk at a lower cost (i.e. 1 packet is £2, 6 packets are £10), and their prices compare very favourably with supermarkets and health shops, although there is a delivery charge on small orders. Delivery takes about 5 days and you are given the opportunity to offset your carbon footprint for £1. **www.ethicalsuperstore. com/category/groceries-and-everyday**

- The Fresh Network supplies raw foods, i.e. which have not been heat-treated in any way, including raw nut butters and oils, olives, sea vegetables, cacao and miso. **www.fresh-network.com/acatalog/index**

- Jekka McVicar grows over 650 varieties of organic herbs at her farm near Bristol and provides seeds and potted plants by mail order. www.jekkasherbfarm.com

- Dried chillies, chipotle paste and powder, tortillas, Mexican oregano and typical Mexican ingredients are available from **www.coolchile.co.uk**

- Dried and fresh chillies, chipotle paste and powder and countless fiery relishes are available from **www.chillipepperpete.co.uk**

- Fresh chillies are available from **www.southdevonchillifarm.co.uk**

- Pomegranate molasses is available from **www.melburyandappleton.co.uk.**

- There are now countless organic box schemes providing fruit and vegetables nationwide, and it is well worth checking out your local ones as the produce will have a low carbon footprint and be very seasonal, as well as cheaper and fresher than supermarkets. I use Riverford Organic Farm, which is based in Devon, and has regional 'sister' farms in different areas. **www.riverford.co.uk**.

Essential equipment

- Sharp knives, and a good sharpening steel, are a must, as vegan cuisine involves a fair amount of chopping.
- Chopping boards.
- Wooden spoons, slotted spoon, spatulas.
- Tin opener.
- Measuring spoons and cups.
- Grater, for ginger and citrus zest – the Microplane ones are excellent, although not cheap.
- Citrus zester, to peel zest off in long strips – Goodgrips works well.
- Vegetable peeler and brush.
- Baking and roasting tins.
- Non-stick frying pans.
- Ridged griddle pan.
- Baking parchment or reusable non-stick oven mats.
- Oven-proof casserole dish.
- Saucepans in all sizes.
- Mixing bowls in all sizes.
- Pastry brushes – the ones with soft, floppy 'bristles' are much better than the ones with densely packed 'hairs'.
- Sturdy blender or food processor.
- Electric mini chopper.
- Electric whisk.
- A food mill such as a Mouli-légumes.
- Pepper grinder.
- Steamer.
- Garlic press.
- Wire whisk.

Forward planning

While deciding what to eat tomorrow or next week today can often take the joyful spontaneity out of cooking and is frequently impractical in our 21st century rushed life style, it is useful as:

- Many pulses require lengthy cooking and it is a good idea to start them off in the morning or even the previous day.
- Many recipes can be broken down into stages, with little effort required at the last moment.

Vegan kitchen hygiene

Meat, fish and eggs are the main culprits in the average kitchen when it comes to bacteria and possible food poisoning. Good hygiene is therefore infinitely easier to apply in the vegan kitchen. There are, however, a few things to remember:

- Wash your hands before handling food.
- Wash fruit and vegetables thoroughly under cold running water.
- Cooked rice can harbour bacteria so refrigerate any leftovers and do not reheat more than once.
- Cool cooked food down completely before refrigerating.
- When reheating cooked food, ensure that it has either come to the boil or is steaming.
- Do not refreeze food which has been thawed unless it has undergone further cooking.
- Separate raw and cooked food in the refrigerator.
- Change dish cloths and tea towels frequently.
- Go through your refrigerator regularly and your store cupboard occasionally and discard anything which is past its sell- or use-by date.

Summing Up

- Keep a well-stocked store cupboard.
- Invest in some quality kitchen equipment.
- Try to plan ahead so that you are not caught short.
- Be aware of basic kitchen hygiene rules.

3

Fruit and Vegetables – Sparkle and Vitality

Organic fruit and vegetables offer us an immeasurable gift in the form of perfect nourishment, of food brimming with natural vitamins, minerals, antioxidants, fibre, enzymes and countless other compounds which all have a part to play in the life of those who eat them. Their contribution to our health and wellbeing must surely be infinite and the role they play in the vegan kitchen lifts them to stardom. When people tell me that they find vegetables boring, I tell them they haven't lived! Take a red pepper for instance. Chop it and toss it into a salad and it offers a crisp, crunchy texture, dazzling colour, and sweet, juicy flavour. Grill it whole until it is soft, blackened and blistered, and it becomes smoky and faintly bitter, soft and silky, deeply seductive and beguiling. Stir-fry it and you get one effect, braise it gently and the result is totally different – so many possibilities wrapped up in just one single vegetable.

Fruit gets a better press than vegetables, but it is often relegated to a very secondary role in the Western diet, eaten as a snack or a way to end a meal, which is a pity as fruit is one of Nature's most delicious foods, bursting with sweetness, fragrance and juice. From the exotic acid tang of a pineapple to the honeyed depth of a Muscat grape and the sharp crispness of an English apple, the range of flavours in the fruits of the world seems almost boundless and their culinary potential is limited only by our creativity and sense of adventure.

In my kitchen, fruit never takes a back seat, as it is an excellent partner to savoury foods, cutting richness, balancing saltiness, bringing out flavour, livening up a sauce or stuffing, or simply adding interest to a plain salad.

Talking of salads, what better way to get 'five-a-day', let alone ten or twelve or twenty, than a salad? Raw food is pure nutrients in their most natural and perfect form, and although some of the components of a salad may be cooked, the high proportion of raw food makes it a nutritional powerhouse as well as a delight to the senses, with its wide range of colours, flavours and textures. Salad possibilities and combinations are endless, and with a bit of imagination, the dreary standard offering of lettuce, cucumber and tomato can be banished forever. Most vegetables can be eaten raw – although some, like broccoli, are rather hard work and therefore not much fun! – and extra nutrients as well as interest can be added in the form of sprouts, nuts, seeds, seaweed flakes, different oils and vinegars, or toasted bread for instance.

Basic Cherry Tomato Salsa

This basic salsa, like the roasted tomato sauce on the next page, is one of the pillars of my vegan cuisine, as it has the ability to dress up a simple dish, giving it sparkle, colour, freshness and interest. It is ready in minutes and if I am looking for a quick and easy lunch, leftover rice, grilled vegetables, corn tortillas or even just a tin of black beans can be given an instant lift. However, you will find that it also crops up in many of the recipes, with specific details of which herb to feature.

Ingredients

50g red onions, peeled and finely chopped
1 garlic clove, peeled and crushed
1 red and 1 green chilli, deseeded and finely sliced
250g cherry tomatoes, quartered – a mixture of red and yellow looks pretty
3 tbsp olive oil
10g any soft, aromatic herb – coriander, parsley, basil, mint, tarragon, dill – coarsely chopped
Sea salt and freshly ground black pepper

Method

Mix all the ingredients gently in a bowl. Season just before serving as salt makes tomatoes watery.

Tip: You can use whatever herb matches the rest of the dish or your mood.

Roasted Tomato Sauce

Although the tomatoes take time to cook, this is an easy sauce to prepare, can be stored in the refrigerator for several days and freezes well.

Tip: Agave nectar is a natural sweetener which has shot to stardom over the last few years due to its favourable performance on the glycemic index. It is sweeter than sugar and can be found in most supermarkets, generally among the sugars rather than cheek by jowl with honey or maple syrup.

Ingredients

1 kg tomatoes, halved
2 tsp agave nectar or runny honey (see tip)
3 tbsp olive oil
6 large garlic cloves, peeled
250g onions, peeled and coarsely chopped
Sea salt and freshly ground black pepper

Method

1. Heat the oven to 200°C/400°F/Gas Mark 6/fan oven 180°C.

2. Put the tomatoes cut side up in a roasting tray lined with foil and drizzle first with agave and then 2 tbsp of olive oil. Season well and cook for 30 minutes. Add the whole garlic cloves and cook for a further 30 minutes, until the tomatoes are soft and slightly blackened.

3. Cool the tomatoes for 10 minutes before transferring, along with the garlic and any juices, to a food processor and processing to a chunky purée.

4. While the tomatoes are roasting, heat the remaining 1 tbsp of olive oil in a frying pan and cook the onions until soft and golden. Add the tomato purée and some seasoning, and cook over medium heat for about 15 minutes, stirring often, until nice and thick.

Pickled Lemons

Jars of these typically Moroccan pickled lemons are available in many supermarkets but they always seem to have a faintly chemical taste. It is well worth making your own as they only take minutes to put together and last virtually indefinitely.

Ingredients

2 organic lemons, scrubbed
75g Maldon salt flakes
Juice of 2 lemons

Method

1 Quarter the lemons and then cut each quarter in half so that you have eight pieces. Layer them up with the salt in a 250ml glass jar and pour in the lemon juice. Cover tightly with a plastic or plastic-coated lid and leave to mature for a minimum of 7 days at room temperature, giving them a good shake every day to redistribute the salt.

2 To use, rinse the lemon pieces well, scrape off and discard the pulp, and dice the skin.

Grilled Peppers

Grilling peppers gives them a faintly smoky flavour and a silky texture. They are available ready grilled in jars in supermarkets but in my opinion they do not compare and it is always worth grilling them at home.

Method

Preheat the grill to high. Line the grill pan with foil, place the peppers on it and grill, about 10cm from the heat and turning as necessary, until black and blistered all over. Cool and use as instructed in the relevant recipe.

Tip: Do not be tempted to use 'coarse' sea salt instead of the Maldon flakes, as they will not dissolve sufficiently to pickle the lemons properly.

Roasted Red Pepper Gazpacho

Serves 2 generously

An Italian version of the ubiquitous Spanish cold soup, more richly flavoured but equally refreshing. Grilling the peppers adds a hint of smokiness while the aromatic pesto fills the whole soup with sunshine and vibrancy. It can also be served hot but be careful not to bring it to boiling point as the olive oil can separate out – aim for nice and steaming.

Tip: One of the most effective ways to grill peppers is to use a blow torch so if you have invested in one for whatever reason, do use it - it is quicker than an electric or gas grill and contributes a whiff of smokiness.

Ingredients

50g wholemeal bread
400g red peppers
1 red, 1 green and 1 yellow pepper, about 200g each
1 garlic clove, peeled
4 tbsp olive oil
175ml water
2 tsp sherry or red wine vinegar
1 x quantity Pesto (page 114)
Sea salt and freshly ground black pepper

Method

1 Place the bread in a shallow bowl and add enough water to saturate it. Set aside to soak.

2 Heat the grill to high. Line the grill pan with foil, arrange all the peppers on it and grill about 10cm from the heat until the skins are black and blistered all over.

3 Cool slightly and remove the skin, seeds and ribs.

4 Dice one red pepper and the yellow and green peppers and set aside.

5 Place the remaining red peppers in a food processor.

6 Squeeze the bread to remove most of the water and add it to the peppers with the garlic. Process until well broken down.

7 With the motor running, slowly add the olive oil and then the water and vinegar.

8 Season to taste, add the diced, roasted peppers and chill.

9 When you are ready to serve, ladle the soup into two bowls and add a good dollop of pesto, adding more as you eat.

Tomato and Orange Soup with a Swirl of Mustard

Serves 2 as a first course

A lovely, fragrant summer soup, perfect for sunny days and lazy lunches in the garden. The tomatoes must be ripe, sweet and juicy to provide the necessary flavour – slightly overripe tomatoes which are going soft and cannot be used in a salad are ideal.

Ingredients

350g ripe tomatoes
1 garlic clove, peeled
1 orange, grated rind and juice
1/8 tsp agave nectar or honey (page 24)
60ml plain soya yoghurt
2 tbsp olive oil
1 x quantity mustard 'mayonnaise' (page 88)
10g chives, finely snipped with scissors
Sea salt and freshly ground black pepper

Method

1 Place the tomatoes, garlic clove, orange juice, agave, 2 tbsp of yoghurt, olive oil and some seasoning in a food processor and process until smooth.

2 Strain through a medium sieve to remove the tomato seeds and bits of skin, then stir in the orange rind and chill.

3 Stir the remaining yoghurt and all but 1 tbsp of chives into the mayonnaise.

4 Stir the soup and check the seasoning, adding a tiny bit more agave if it is too sharp. Ladle into two bowls and swirl in a good spoonful of the mustard mayonnaise.

5 Sprinkle with the reserved chives and serve.

Tip: I like to leave tomatoes in a bowl on the window sill where they can catch some sun, a trick I learned from the head gardener at West Dean Gardens in West Sussex some years ago when I was researching an article on tomatoes – a few days in the sun really makes a difference to the flavour.

Double Beetroot Soup

Serves 4

Beetroot is not an elegant vegetable. Bulbous and lurid, its appearance is somewhat at odds with its sweet, earthy flavour which speaks not of flamboyance but of flatness and insipidity. On its own, it turns few heads, but its deeply hued flesh, whether magenta or gold, starts to shine when it is partnered with acid ingredients like citrus, vinegar or green apples which quench the sweetness and bring out its fruity, caramel tones.

Tip: Golden beetroot is available in some supermarkets but the best place to find it is in an organic vegetable box or a farmers' market. Its flavour is no different but its warm, golden colouring is a wonderful contrast in this soup.

Ingredients

2 tbsp olive oil
225g red onions, peeled and coarsely chopped
750g red beetroot, peeled and diced
2 sharp eating apples, about 250g, peeled, cored and diced
1 tbsp bouillon powder
1/2 tsp balsamic vinegar
250g golden beetroot, cooked, skinned and diced
Seeds from 1 small pomegranate (see tip on page 62)
50g red onions, peeled and finely chopped
1 lime, juiced
1 green chilli, deseeded and finely sliced
50g walnut pieces, toasted
10g fresh coriander, coarsely chopped
250ml plain soya yoghurt, well seasoned (page 52)
Sea salt and freshly ground black pepper

Method

1   Heat 1 tbsp of oil in a medium saucepan, add the onions and cook gently, stirring occasionally, until translucent, about 10 minutes. Stir in the red beetroot and apples and cook for a further 5 minutes.

2   Pour in enough water to cover the vegetables by 5cm, sprinkle in the bouillon powder, vinegar and some seasoning, cover the pan and simmer until the beetroot is totally soft – this can take up to an hour.

3   While the soup is cooking, mix the golden beetroot, pomegranate seeds, finely chopped onions, lime juice, chilli and remaining olive oil in a bowl. Add the walnuts, coriander and some seasoning just before serving.

4   Blend the soup until it is totally smooth – and if you have the time and inclination, pass it through a medium mesh sieve to give it a wonderfully velvety texture. Check the seasoning.

5   Ladle the soup into four warm bowls, swirl a dollop of yoghurt into it and spoon some of the beetroot and pomegranate relish into the centre.

6   Serve immediately, although the soup can be refrigerated overnight and eaten chilled.

Tomato Chutney and Basil Bruschetta

Makes 4 bruschette

This chutney is the ideal solution for dealing with tomatoes which are passed their salad best and too soft for anything else. Although it requires fairly lengthy cooking, it can be left on a back burner to simmer away quietly – but do watch it towards the end of its cooking time, as it goes bitter if it scorches.

Ingredients

4 tbsp olive oil
250g red onions, peeled and coarsely chopped
3 garlic cloves, peeled and crushed
750g tomatoes, coarsely chopped
1 tbsp balsamic vinegar
1/2 tsp chipotle chilli powder or paste (see tip)
4 sliced of wholemeal bread, toasted
1 x quantity pesto (page 114)
Dressed salad leaves, to serve (optional)
Sea salt and freshly ground black pepper

Method

1   Heat the olive oil in a large deep frying pan, add the onions and garlic, and cook over medium heat, stirring often, until they are golden.

2   Tip in the tomatoes, vinegar, chilli and some salt, turn the heat right down, and leave to cook, stirring every now and then, until the mixture is thick and most of the tomato moisture has evaporated. Allow to cool.

3   Spread the bread with the chutney and spoon the pesto over the top.

4   Serve immediately with some salad leaves.

Tip: 7/10 on the heat scale, the chipotle is a smoked, dried jalapeño, rich and hot, with a distinctive flavour and hints of tobacco and chocolate. The paste and powder are available in some supermarkets and by mail order.

Griddled Ratatouille Salad

Serves 4 as a side dish or first course

Ratatolha, as it was called in the old Langue d'Oc, comes in many guises. Every chef, let alone every housewife, has a recipe which is the 'one and only', 'totally authentic', 'passed down through countless generations in my family', etc. It can certainly vary from one restaurant to another, and from one village to another, but the basics are fairly reliable. It is the quintessential Provençal recipe, bursting with Mediterranean flavours, and its versatility is one of its charms. It is normally served hot, but in my opinion, it is even better cold, well doused in extra virgin olive oil and topped with a handful of shredded basil.

Tip: This salad is easy to make, but griddling the vegetables takes time, so save it for a day when there are not too many other pressures.

Ingredients

1 small ciabatta loaf, cut into 2cm pieces
6 tbsp olive oil plus extra for brushing
2 garlic cloves, peeled and crushed
1 tbsp dried Herbes de Provence (page 175)
1 large red pepper, about 250g
1 large yellow or orange pepper, about 250g
250g aubergines, washed
350g courgettes, washed
150g red onions
1 large organic lemon, scrubbed
1 tsp smooth Dijon mustard
15g flat leaf parsley, coarsely chopped
200g small tomatoes, halved
100g pitted black olives
15g basil, shredded
Sea salt and freshly ground black pepper

Method

1   Preheat the oven to 200°C/400°F/Gas Mark 6/fan oven 180°C.

2   Place the ciabatta pieces in a roasting tin and toss them with 2 tbsp of olive oil, a crushed garlic clove, the Herbes de Provence and some salt. Bake for about 10 minutes, stirring once or twice, until they are golden and crunchy. The croûtons can be made well ahead of time and stored in an airtight container.

3   Heat a ridged griddle pan over medium heat until good and hot.

4   Pour some olive oil into a cup, brush the peppers with it, and place them on the griddle. Leave them to cook undisturbed for about 10 minutes, until they start to soften. Turn them over and cook them on all sides until they are fairly soft all over. Cool, then peel, remove the stem, seeds and ribs, and cut into 1cm wide slices. Place in a wide deep serving dish

5   While the peppers are cooking, top and tail the aubergines and cut them lengthways into slices about 5mm thick, discarding the first and last slices which will be nothing but skin.

6   Brush both sides with olive oil and arrange them on the griddle. Season them and leave them to cook for about 5 minutes, until the underside is nicely striped. Carefully turn them over, season them again and cook the other side in the same way.

7   Remove the aubergines to a plate.

8   Prepare the courgettes in the same way while the aubergine is cooking: top and tail them, slice them lengthways, again discarding the end slices, brush with olive oil and season. Cook on the griddle when the aubergines are done.

9   Top and tail the unpeeled onions and cut them into rounds about 1cm thick. Brush them with olive oil and cook them on the griddle. They will take slightly longer than the aubergine and courgettes, about 7 minutes on the first side and 4 on the second. Remove and discard the skins.

10 Make the dressing while you are waiting for the vegetables to cook. With a lemon zester, peel the zest from the lemon in long strips, wrap in cling film or damp kitchen paper, and set aside. If you do not have a lemon zester, simply skip this step.

11 Juice the lemon, measure out 2 tbsp and whisk in a small bowl with 4 tbsp of olive oil, a crushed garlic clove, the mustard, parsley and some seasoning.

12 When the aubergines, courgettes and onions are ready, add them with the croûtons to the peppers, spoon over the dressing, and mix *very* gently – hands are best for this.

13 And finally the tomatoes: brush them with olive oil, season and cook cut side down on the griddle for about 5 minutes, until they start to caramelise. Carefully turn them over and cook the skin side for a further 5 minutes.

14 Arrange the tomatoes on top of the other vegetables in the serving dish.

15 Set the salad aside for half an hour to allow the flavours to blend and the croûtons to soften.

16 Sprinkle the salad with the lemon zest, olives and basil and serve.

French Bean and Roast Tomato Salad with Garlicky Breadcrumbs

Serves 2

Tomatoes can be friend or foe. If they have been allowed to ripen on the vine and enjoy plenty of sunshine and warmth, they are sweet, juicy, aromatic, perfect. But more often than not, they have been picked while unripe, left to languish for days if not weeks in a stark, refrigerated environment, and shipped all over the place – and they are hard, woolly, tasteless, a huge disappointment. However, all is not lost! Roasting even the dreariest tomato with garlic and olive oil will turn it into the belle of the ball, giving it softness, chewiness, caramelised sweetness, mellow sharpness, in fact assets galore.

Tip: The tomatoes can be cooked the day before and refrigerated. Bring them back to room temperature before assembling the salad.

Ingredients

375g tomatoes, halved
5 tbsp olive oil
1 tbsp agave nectar or runny honey (page 24)
100g soft, wholemeal breadcrumbs
1 garlic clove, peeled and crushed
250g French beans, topped, tailed and halved
25g pine nuts, toasted (page 86)
25g red onions, peeled and thinly sliced
15g basil leaves, roughly torn
Sea salt and freshly ground black pepper

Method

1   Preheat the oven to 200°C/400°F/Gas Mark 6/fan oven 180°C.

2   Arrange the tomatoes on a foil-lined baking tray, drizzle with 1 tbsp of olive oil and the agave, and season well. Bake on the top shelf of the oven for about one hour, until they are slightly wizened and blackened along the edges. Allow to cool.

3   Place the breadcrumbs in a roasting tray, stir in 1 tbsp of olive oil and the crushed garlic and spread out into a thin layer.

4   Bake on the middle shelf of the oven, under the tomatoes, for 10 to 15 minutes, stirring once or twice, until they are crisp and golden. Allow to cool.

5   Cook the French beans in plenty of boiling, salted water for about 3 minutes until crisp and tender, drain and refresh under cold running water. Drain again and shake out any remaining moisture. Wrap them in a clean tea towel to dry them out totally.

6 When you are ready to serve, toss the French beans, pine nuts, red onions, basil and some seasoning in a bowl with the remaining olive oil. Divide between two plates, arrange the tomatoes on top and sprinkle with the breadcrumbs.

7 Serve immediately.

Beurre De Provence

Serves 2

The olive groves of southern France are renowned for the intensely fruity, dark green olive oil they produce which is combined in this recipe with an unquestionable abundance of roasted garlic to make a thick, unctuous, fabulously fragrant, very Mediterranean 'butter'. It is not for the squeamish and probably not the best thing to serve to elderly relatives, but if garlic is an essential part of your life, you have just hit the jackpot!

Ingredients

325g garlic cloves, 5 to 9 heads of garlic
175ml olive oil
Crudités, marinated black olives and thin slices of French bread, brushed with olive oil and grilled, to serve
Sea salt and freshly ground black pepper

Method

1 Give the garlic cloves a good whack with something solid like a tin of tomatoes, a rolling pin or a jar of honey, and peel. Place in an ovenproof china dish, pour in the oil and cover tightly with foil.

2 Cook in a preheated oven at 150°C/300°F/Gas Mark 2/fan oven 125°C for one and a half hours, by which time the garlic should be soft and golden. Add some seasoning and purée in a food processor before pushing through a medium mesh sieve.

3 Leave to cool and check the seasoning.

4 Serve at room temperature with a selection of raw vegetables, some olives and grilled bread.

Tip: Bashing the garlic cloves loosens the skins and makes them easy to remove, but this method does result in smelly fingers which need to be rubbed with a cut lemon to freshen them.

Stuffed Peppers

Serves 2 for lunch with a salad

Za'atar is a popular Middle Eastern condiment, herby and nutty. While recipes and ingredients vary, it usually contains dried aromatic herbs like thyme, oregano and marjoram and sesame seeds or pine nuts. Spices like fennel and cumin are sometimes added, and many mixtures are quite heavily salted. It is often simply sprinkled over food to give an extra layer of flavour, but in the filling for these peppers, it stays well in the background, providing almost more of an aroma than actually contributing to the taste. Za'atar is available in some supermarkets and from Seasoned Pioneers (page 17).

Tip: If you prefer, the peppers can be served at room temperature, and they are also very good cold the following day.

Ingredients

3 tbsp olive oil plus extra for drizzling
150g onions, peeled and coarsely chopped
2 garlic cloves, peeled and crushed
400g aubergines, peeled and diced
1 tbsp za'atar (see above)
1 tsp bouillon powder
250g tomatoes, coarsely chopped
25g raisins
2 tbsp thyme leaves, coarsely chopped
25g sunflower seeds, toasted (page 86)
1 x quantity nut cheese made with cashews (page 87)
1 red and 1 yellow pepper, about 200g each
4 bay leaves
4 thin slices of lemon
Sea salt and freshly ground black pepper

Method

1 Heat 3 tbsp of oil in a medium frying pan, add the onions and garlic and cook gently, stirring every now and then, until translucent. Add the aubergines and continue to cook until everything is soft and golden.

2 Remove from the heat and stir in the za'atar, bouillon, tomatoes, raisins, thyme, sunflower seeds and some seasoning. Cool slightly before folding in the cashew cheese.

3 Preheat the oven to 200°C/400°F/Gas Mark 6/fan oven 180°C.

4 Cut the peppers in half lengthways, right through the stem, and remove the core, seeds and ribs – leave the stem in place as it helps the pepper halves to keep their shape. Place in a baking dish where they fit snugly.

5 Season with salt and pepper, and divide the vegetable mixture between them. Place a bay leaf on each pepper half and top with a slice of lemon. Drizzle liberally with olive oil.

6 Cover the dish securely with kitchen foil and bake for one hour. Remove the foil and cook for a further 15 minutes.

7 To test if the peppers are done, gently squeeze them. If they still feel slightly hard, return them to the oven for a further 10 minutes; if the peppers are particularly fleshy and therefore thicker, they may need to bake a bit longer.

8 To serve, place two pepper halves on two warm plates and drizzle over any juices which have accumulated in the dish.

Middle Eastern Pitta Bread Casserole

Serves 4

This casserole is faintly reminiscent of lasagne, with spicy, tomatoey chickpeas layered with toasted pitta bread and baked until crusty and golden. It is a substantial dish, with successive bursts of flavour provided by the spices, raisins, yoghurt and coriander. Ras el hanout can be quite sweet, depending on the brand, so start off with 1 tbsp and taste again before assembling the casserole, adding a bit more if it is not quite fragrant and aromatic enough for you.

Ingredients

4 wholemeal pitta breads, torn into 4 cm pieces
2 tbsp olive oil
400g onions, peeled and thinly sliced
3 garlic cloves, peeled and crushed
1 tbsp cumin seeds, toasted and coarsely ground (page 86)
1 tbsp ras el hanout or to taste (see above)
50g raisins
2 x 400g tinned chopped tomatoes
2 x 400g tinned chickpeas, rinsed and drained
1 tbsp bouillon powder
30 black olives, pitted and halved
2 tbsp capers, rinsed and squeezed dry
1/4 tsp saffron threads
500ml plain soya yoghurt
25g pine nuts
10g fresh coriander, coarsely chopped
Sea salt and freshly ground black pepper
3.5pt soufflé dish

Tip: Although I normally serve this casserole hot, with a salad, the cold leftovers are terribly good the following day, if somewhat solid, particularly as picnic food or on a long hike when your energy needs replenishing - but if you are carrying it in a rucksack, make sure you pack it very carefully, as the juices tend to leak out of the most hermetic container, so wrap it in several sheets of cling film.

Method

1 Preheat the oven to 200°C/400°F/Gas Mark 6/fan oven 180°C. Spread the pitta bread out on a baking tray and toast it for about 10 minutes, until it is dry and crisp.

2 Heat the olive oil in a large saucepan, add the onions and garlic, and cook over gentle heat, stirring occasionally, until soft and golden. Sprinkle in the spices and some seasoning, and stir-fry for a minute or two.

3 Stir in the raisins, tomatoes, chickpeas and bouillon, raise the heat to medium, and cook for about 10 minutes, until some of the moisture has evaporated. Fold in the olives, capers and saffron, and check the seasoning.

4 Place half the chickpea mixture in a three and a half pint soufflé dish. Cover with half the pitta bread, and then spoon over half the yoghurt. Repeat the process to make a second layer. Sprinkle the pine nuts over the yoghurt.

5 Preheat the oven to 200°C/400°F/Gas Mark 6/fan oven 180°C and bake the casserole for 20 to 30 minutes, until the juices are bubbling and the pine nuts are golden.

6 Leave the casserole to rest for 10 minutes, sprinkle with coriander and serve immediately.

Summer Vegetable Salad with Dill Dressing

Serves 2

There is a small window of opportunity between spring and summer which is very rewarding: asparagus are nearing the end of their brief spell but are still plentiful and considerably cheaper, and the first young peas and broad beans, tender and sweet, are trickling in. Their flavours are all so wonderfully seasonal that I find myself visiting the green grocer virtually on a daily basis to take advantage of them and feature them in whatever I am cooking: soups, risottos, and salads like this one. Admittedly, there is a certain amount of shelling involved, so I become rather self-centred at this time of the year and ensure that I am cooking for no more than two!

Ingredients

8 very thin slices plain ciabatta
1/2 tsp dried dill weed
Olive oil for brushing and 120ml
600g broad beans, shelled
250g peas, shelled
1 bunch, about 20, slender asparagus spears, trimmed
150g cucumber
1 large orange, washed
15g fresh dill
1 garlic clove, peeled
1 tbsp capers, rinsed and squeezed dry
1 tsp wholegrain mustard
4 spring onions, trimmed and finely sliced
Sea salt and freshly ground black pepper

Method

1 Preheat the oven to 160°C/325°F/Gas Mark 3/fan oven 145°C.

2 Lay the ciabatta slices out on a baking tray, brush with olive oil and sprinkle with dill weed. Bake for about 10 minutes until light gold. Set aside to cool.

3 Cook the beans, peas and asparagus separately in plenty of boiling salted water. The time will depend on their age, so test after 5 minutes.

4 Drain and refresh them in turn under cold running water.

Tip: While fresh broad beans and peas are an absolute joy, the frozen varieties do actually work quite well in this salad and save an awful lot of time, although frozen broad beans definitely have to be skinned. The asparagus, however, must be fresh and British.

5 If the broad beans are large, slip them out of their jackets as they will be tough – boring I know but it does not take long with this quantity.

6 Place all the vegetables in a clean tea towel and set them aside to dry out a bit.

7 Halve the cucumber lengthways and, with a melon baller or small teaspoon, scrape out the seeds which are watery. Slice the cucumber on the diagonal about 3mm thick.

8 With a citrus zester, remove the zest from the orange in long thin strips before squeezing the juice.

9 In a food processor, blend the orange juice, dill, garlic, capers, mustard, 120ml of olive oil and some salt and pepper, until you have a thick, smooth dressing. Check the seasoning.

10 Gently toss the asparagus, broad beans, peas, cucumber, spring onions and orange zest in a salad bowl. Add the dressing and toss again. Divide between two plates and top with the crisp ciabatta.

11 Serve immediately.

Sopas Mallorquinas

Serves 2 as a main dish

Although 'sopas' means soups in Spanish, in Mallorca it is the name given to thin slices of stale bread, which are often used to add body and bulk to other dishes. In the case of Sopas Mallorquinas, which are not a soup at all, vegetables in broth are ladled over bread, creating a thick, savoury stew – definitely peasant food, hearty and rib-sticking. Greens such as chard and cabbage are traditional, although I prefer to use spinach as it results in a lighter, fresher tasting and looking dish. The bread has to be dense so don't try to make the sopas with sliced supermarket bread: pain de campagne, sourdough or a good heavy wholemeal loaf are ideal.

Tip: Pimentón is a Spanish paprika with wonderfully smoky undertones. The sweeter pimentón dulce is quite mild, while pimentón picante is much spicier and hotter. It is available in many large supermarkets and delicatessens, or by mail order.

Ingredients

125g stale bread, thinly sliced
2 tbsp olive oil
275g onions, peeled and coarsely chopped
3 garlic cloves, peeled and crushed
1 small red or yellow pepper, about 175g, cut into pieces
375g tomatoes, skinned and chopped
1 tsp sweet smoked paprika (pimentón dulce) (see tip)
750ml vegetable stock – water mixed with bouillon powder is fine
200g baby spinach leaves, washed
2 tbsp chopped parsley
Sea salt and freshly ground black pepper

Method

1 Heat the oven to its lowest setting. Spread the sliced bread out on a baking tray and put it in the oven to dry out and crisp.

2 Heat the oil in a saucepan, add the onions, garlic and pepper, and cook, stirring occasionally, until they are soft and starting to brown.

3 Add the tomatoes, paprika and some seasoning, and stir-fry for five minutes.

4 Pour in the stock, bring to the boil, and simmer for 10 minutes.

5 Add the spinach and cook for a minute or two, until it is just wilted. Check the seasoning.

6 Place the bread in two deep plates and ladle the vegetable broth over it.

7 Sprinkle with parsley and serve immediately.

Root Vegetable Mash with Shallots in Red Wine

Serves 4

The vegetable box which arrives on our doorstep every Friday can be a bit of a challenge during the winter, with its regular crop of mud-caked root vegetables, but it certainly gets my creativity flowing as I rack my brains and imagination for different ways to serve them. This mash is an excellent solution, as it takes care of the celeriac, parsnips and swedes all in one go!

Ingredients

4 tbsp and 120ml olive oil
500g each celeriac, parsnips and swedes, peeled and cut into 2cm pieces
400g shallots or button onions, peeled
100ml red wine
100ml vegetable stock or water with 1 tsp bouillon powder
1 tbsp grenadine syrup (see tip)
50g pecans, toasted and coarsely chopped (page 86)
Sea salt and freshly ground black pepper

Method

1 Heat 2 tbsp of olive oil in a large heavy saucepan and, when it starts to sizzle, add the vegetables, cover the pan and leave to cook gently, stirring often and scraping the bottom well, until they are soft and golden in places. This will take 30 to 40 minutes.

2 Transfer the vegetables to a food processor, add 120ml of olive oil and some seasoning, and process until smooth.

3 While the vegetables are cooking, heat the remaining 2 tbsp of oil in a medium frying pan, add the shallots and cook them over medium heat, stirring occasionally until they are golden all over, about 20 minutes.

4 Pour in the red wine, stock and grenadine and cook fairly briskly until there are only two or three tablespoons of liquid left.

5 Turn the heat right down and continue to cook, stirring often, until the liquid is reduced to a thick syrup and coats the shallots nicely.

6 Reheat the mash if necessary and divide it between four warm plates. Spoon the shallots and their syrup over it.

7 Sprinkle with pecans and serve immediately.

Tip:
Grenadine syrup is a popular cocktail ingredient and is available in most large supermarkets. In this dish, it adds both colour and a hint of exoticism to the shallots.

Pasta Shells with Sweet Potatoes, Mushrooms and Walnuts

Serves 4

Tip:
Sage, like rosemary and thyme, is a very aromatic herb, particularly when used raw, and a little goes a long way. It gives this dressing just enough sharpness to balance the sweetness of the potatoes.

Sweet potatoes can be rather bland and insipid but pan- or oven-roasting them with some oil concentrates their sweetness and gives them some sparkle. In this easy dish, they are combined with meaty portabello mushrooms, fresh herbs and toasted walnuts to make a richly flavoured dressing for pasta shells.

Ingredients

3 tbsp and 120ml olive oil
200g red onions, peeled and coarsely chopped
350g sweet potatoes, peeled and cut into 2cm cubes
200g portabello mushrooms, peeled and thickly sliced
1 garlic clove, peeled
25g flat leaf parsley
25g fresh sage
2 tbsp capers, rinsed and squeezed dry
1 tbsp red wine vinegar
1 tbsp wholegrain mustard
250g wholewheat pasta shells
75g walnuts, toasted and coarsely chopped (page 86)
Sea salt and freshly ground black pepper

Method

1   Heat the 3 tbsp of olive oil in a medium saucepan and add the onions and sweet potatoes. Cook over medium heat, stirring occasionally, until they just start to brown.

2   Add the mushrooms and some seasoning, cover the pan, turn the heat right down and leave to cook for about 30 minutes, by which time the potatoes will be soft.

3   Uncover the pan, turn the heat up to medium and continue to cook until all the moisture from the mushrooms has evaporated.

4   While the vegetables are cooking, blend the garlic, herbs, capers, vinegar, mustard, remaining oil and some seasoning in a food processor to make a bright green vinaigrette.

5 Cook the pasta shells according to the manufacturer's instructions, drain well and return to the pan. Scrape the vegetable mixture on top of the pasta, sprinkle in the walnuts and stir everything together very gently so as not to mash the potatoes.

6 Divide the pasta between four warm plates, spoon the herb vinaigrette over the top and serve immediately.

Turkish Stuffed Artichokes

Serves 2

Globe artichokes are one of my favourite summer vegetables. Although wizened, bruised and tired-looking specimens can occasionally be found throughout the year, they are truly seasonal and hard to come by outside the summer months. So when the first young and modest specimens appear at the green grocers or in my organic box, a thrill of anticipation sends me skipping to the kitchen to develop a new recipe or renew my close friendship with one from last year or even further back. I start off by simply steaming them and eating them hot, leaf by leaf, with olive oil. As they become more plentiful and the season progresses, I look for suitable partners to show off their fairly delicate but glorious flavour. The following recipe is for mid or late season artichokes, as they need to be big and blowsy, providing plenty of room for the gutsy stuffing.

Tip: Artichoke leaves can be thorny and therefore need to be handled carefully. Snipping the spiky tips off with scissors is a good solution and improves the presentation, but it is time-consuming!

Ingredients

2 large globe artichokes
3 tbsp olive oil
125g onions, peeled and chopped
225g tomatoes, skinned and coarsely chopped
15g pine nuts, toasted (page 86)
50g soft wholemeal breadcrumbs
10 black olives, pitted and quartered
1 bushy sprig of fresh rosemary, needles finely chopped
1 tbsp pomegranate molasses
5g parsley, finely chopped
Sea salt and freshly ground black pepper

Method

1   Snap the stalks off the artichokes and either steam or boil for about 40 minutes, until a leaf from the centre comes out easily. Leave them to cool upside down so that they drain completely.

2   Heat 1 tbsp of olive oil in a small frying pan. Add the onions and cook over medium heat, stirring occasionally, until soft and golden, about 20 minutes. Stir in the tomatoes and cook for 10 minutes longer, until the tomatoes are softened but not mushy.

3   Cool slightly and stir in the pine nuts, breadcrumbs, olives, rosemary, molasses, parsley and some seasoning.

4 Remove most of the leaves from the centre of the artichokes, leaving just two or three outer layers to form a container. Scrape out the choke with a teaspoon.

5 Preheat the oven to 200°C/400°F/Gas Mark 6/fan oven 180°C. Place the artichokes in a roasting tin and spoon the stuffing into them. Drizzle the remaining olive oil over them, cover the tin with foil and bake for 30 minutes.

6 Remove the foil and cook for a further 10 minutes.

7 Serve immediately.

Portabello Mushroom Burgers

Serves 2

Portabello mushrooms come in different sizes, from barely 4cm across to giant specimens which can weigh almost half a pound. They are simply an adult brown mushroom and acquire not only bulk but depth of flavour as they grow to maturity. Their firm, meaty texture makes them an excellent choice for stuffing and for stewing, and in this recipe, they provide a welcome chewiness.

Ingredients

Tip:
Peeling the mushrooms exposes the white, porous flesh of the cap, which enables it to absorb moisture and flavour.

1 small red and 1 small yellow pepper, about 150g each, cut into 1cm strips
175g red onions, peeled and thickly sliced
3 tbsp olive oil
1 sprig of fresh rosemary, needles finely chopped
2 large portabello mushrooms, peeled
2 hamburger buns
1 x quantity mustard 'mayonnaise' (page 88)
Sea salt and freshly ground black pepper

Method

1 Preheat the oven to 200°C/400°F/Gas Mark 6/fan oven180°C.

2 Toss the peppers and onions together in a baking dish with 1 tbsp of olive oil and some seasoning. Bake on the top shelf, stirring occasionally, until soft and just starting to blacken along the edges, about 30 minutes. Stir in the rosemary and keep warm.

3 Place the mushrooms gill side up in a baking dish where they fit snugly. Season, drizzle with 1 tbsp of olive oil and bake in the oven on the shelf below the peppers until soft and cooked through, about 20 minutes.

4 Split the buns and toast the cut side. Place the bottom halves on 2 warm plates, top with a mushroom, then divide the mustard mayonnaise between them.

5 Spoon the peppers and onions over everything and drizzle with the remaining tbsp of olive oil.

6 Serve immediately.

Leek and Potato Purée

Serves 4 as a side dish

Despite the small amount of oil, this purée has a wonderful depth of flavour and a sweet richness which is positively addictive. Leeks are difficult to quantify as the coarse, green proportion varies, so choose ready trimmed leeks where most of the green top has been removed.

Ingredients

4 tbsp olive oil
650g leeks, trimmed weight, washed and coarsely chopped
12 garlic cloves, peeled
1kg potatoes, peeled and cut into 3cm pieces
Sea salt and freshly ground black pepper

Method

1   Heat the oil in a saucepan, add the leeks and garlic, cover and leave to sweat on low heat, stirring occasionally, for about 30 minutes, until the leeks are totally soft. Remove the lid, turn the heat up to medium and cook until most of the moisture has evaporated.

2   While the leeks are cooking, bring a large pot of salted water to the boil, add the potatoes and cook until tender, about 15 minutes. Drain well and mash with a potato masher or ricer.

3   Place the leeks in food processor with some seasoning and process until smooth. Add the mashed potatoes and process again for a few seconds, just until it is all amalgamated. Scrape back into the saucepan and check the seasoning. Reheat if necessary and serve immediately.

Tip: Leeks can harbour grit deep in their layers and the best way to ensure they are clean is to split them half way down before washing under cold running water.

Pears Poached in Summer Berry Syrup

Serves 4

The raspberry purée turns these pears the most wonderful glowing magenta and yet does not overpower their delicate flavour. The poaching liquid, strained and flavoured with Crème de Framboise, is poured over the pears, and the end result is a spectacular pudding for late summer or early autumn. All the poaching and preparation can be done well ahead of time and the pears left to chill in the refrigerator until you are ready to serve.

Tip: It is important, I think, to serve any kind of poached pear on a slightly larger plate than usual, as separating the flesh from the core is challenging, which can mean bright pink syrup splashing all over the dinner table!

Ingredients

500g frozen raspberries or mixed summer berries, defrosted
4 large ripe Comice or King William pears with stems
250g caster sugar
500ml water
2 tbsp Crème de Framboise or Cassis liqueur
Vegan cream or ice cream, to serve (optional)

Method

1 Place the berries and any juices in a food processor and process to a smooth purée. Press the purée through a medium mesh nylon or stainless steel sieve to remove the pips.

2 Peel the pears, leaving the stems intact, and scoop out the blossom end with a small spoon or melon baller.

3 Mix the fruit purée, caster sugar and water in a saucepan large enough to fit the pears fairly snugly. Add the pears, which should be totally covered with liquid – if they are not, pour in enough water to cover them. Bring to the boil on medium heat, then turn the heat right down and leave the pears to cook very gently in the syrup until they are tender and translucent. Remove the saucepan from the heat and set it all aside until everything is cool – overnight is ideal.

4 With a slotted spoon, remove the pears from the liquid, set them upright in a deep container and place them in the refrigerator.

5 Strain the cooking liquid through a fine sieve into a saucepan, bring to the boil, and simmer until well reduced and syrupy. Stir in the Framboise and leave to cool.

6 Pour over the pears and return them to the refrigerator until you are ready to serve.

7 Place the pears on individual plates, spoon the sauce over them and serve immediately.

Beaumes de Venise Jelly with Grape and Banana Salad

Serves 4

Grapes and wine are an obvious partnership, and a sweet wine like Beaumes de Venise from Provence, with its exquisitely honeyed, Muscat flavour, makes a heavenly, boozy jelly.

Ingredients

4 x 100ml (or thereabouts) metal ramekins, brushed with flavourless oil
100g caster sugar
100ml water
350ml and 4 tbsp Beaumes de Venise wine
1 sachet Vege-Gel (see tip on page 122)
3 tsp fresh lemon juice
100g each black and white seedless grapes, halved
2 large ripe bananas, peeled and thinly sliced
50g toasted, flaked almonds
Vegan cream or ice cream, to serve (optional)

Tip: Sauternes is also an excellent choice for a jelly, but it is more expensive.

Method

1   Chill the ramekins in the refrigerator.

2   Place the sugar and water in a small saucepan and bring to the boil, stirring to dissolve the sugar. Cool for 10 minutes before adding the 350ml of wine and 2 tsp of lemon juice. Sprinkle over the Vege-Gel and stir until it is totally dissolved. Heat until just below boiling point, stirring constantly, and strain into a jug. Pour into the ramekins, place in the refrigerator and chill for several hours or overnight until set. Bring back to room temperature before serving.

3   To make the fruit salad, place the grapes and bananas in a bowl, drizzle with the 4 tbsp of wine and remaining lemon juice and toss gently. Sprinkle with almonds just before serving.

4   Un-mould the jellies by dipping the ramekins very briefly in hot water. Turn out on to plates.

5   Serve the jellies with the fruit salad.

Pulses and Grains – Comfort and Joy

Packed with protein, complex carbohydrates and fibre, pulses and grains are the comfort food of the vegan kitchen, as well as the engine room, providing slow-release, steady energy. They feature widely in all ethnic cuisines, and in many countries where so many cannot afford to eat meat and fish, they take centre stage as the principal component of the meal.

Pulses come in all shapes, sizes and colours, from the tiny slate green Puy lentil, with its very own Appellation d'Origine Contrôlée (AOC), to the big fat butter bean which breaks down into a magically velvety texture. They all have their own very specific, individual flavour but equally importantly, they excel at absorbing the essence of other ingredients like oils, vinegars, herbs and spices. I never soak beans, as I find it affects the end flavour and texture – it is much better to cook them long and slow, and a bay leaf or strip of kombu seaweed does wonders to reduce their windiness!

The soy bean is in a class of its own, in that it is a complete protein, but as far as I am concerned, there its talents end! Its flavour is far from pronounced and its texture unpleasantly mealy, but there are several soy bean products which can be useful in the vegan kitchen: soy sauce, soya milk and yoghurt, miso, tofu, seitan and tempeh, and while these last two feature only very occasionally in my cooking, the others do have an important role to play:

Soy sauce

Soy sauce varies in quality, saltiness and taste, and my favourites are Clearspring's Organic Tamari, which is wheat-free, and shoyu. Nama shoyu is an unpasteurised soy sauce and well worth the investment.

Soya yoghurt

Plain soya yoghurt is rather bland and needs to be well seasoned with salt and pepper and sharpened with plenty of lemon juice. It also benefits from the addition of extra virgin olive oil if it is being served on its own. Some brands are quite sweet – my favourites are Sojade and Provamel. While soya yoghurt acts as an ingredient in some of my recipes, I love it as an accompaniment to a dish, to provide sharpness, moisture and a change of texture.

Miso

Miso comes in different strengths and types, and is made essentially from soya beans and grains which are fermented for anything from one to six years. The most common are red miso, high in protein; white miso, high in carbohydrates and therefore quite sweet and mild; barley miso, rich and salty, and soy miso, hearty and nourishing.

Tofu

Tofu has a bad reputation, which is well deserved as it has no flavour whatsoever. However, it does have its uses. Silken tofu breaks down into a rich, creamy texture, while regular tofu is good where a crumbled or mashed effect is sought.

Grains

Grains are perhaps not as versatile or numerous as pulses, but the variety is considerably greater than most people realise. We are all familiar with rice and wheat, and corn to a lesser extent, but quinoa, millet, amaranth, barley and buckwheat (actually a grass rather than a grain) are all well worth some experimenting, particularly quinoa for its very high protein content.

Chickpea and Pitta Salad

Serves 4 as a light lunch

This is a quick and easy salad to put together, fresh and bright, gutsy, full of summer flavours and aromas, perfect for lunch in the garden – but don't hesitate to serve it in winter as well, to remind yourself of warm Mediterranean sun and chase away the blues: just plunge the drained chickpeas into a saucepan of boiling water and leave them to heat up for 5 minutes. I tend to use a mixture of red and yellow cherry tomatoes in this salad, but any kind of tomato works well, from thickly sliced beef tomatoes to quartered plum tomatoes.

Ingredients

1 large wholemeal pitta bread
1 lemon, washed
100g cucumber (a piece about 7cm long), seeded and diced
1 x 400g tin chickpeas, rinsed and well drained
100g cherry tomatoes, quartered
40g red onions, peeled and finely chopped
1 garlic clove, peeled and crushed
4 tbsp olive oil
40g pitted black olives, halved
10g mint, coarsely chopped
10g flat leaf parsley, coarsely chopped
Sea salt and freshly ground black pepper

Method

1   Preheat the oven to 160°C/325°F/Gas Mark 3/fan oven 145°C.

2   Cut the pitta bread into 2cm pieces with scissors or a bread knife. Spread out on a baking tray and bake in the oven until they are dry and crisp, about 20 minutes.

3   With a lemon zester, peel long strips of zest from the lemon. If you don't have a zester, grate the zest finely. Squeeze the juice from the lemon.

4   Toss the cucumber, lemon zest and juice, chickpeas, tomatoes, onions, garlic, olive oil and olives together in a salad bowl.

5   Add the herbs, some seasoning and the pitta bread, and stir gently.

6   Set aside for 10 minutes before serving so that the pitta absorbs some of the olive oil and juice from the tomatoes.

Tip: Tins of chickpeas are a great standby in the kitchen as they can be turned into a nourishing and satisfying meal without too much effort or too many other ingredients, while the dried ones take hours to cook and never seem to become soft enough.

Cretan Split Pea Soup with Skordalia and Greek Salata

Serves 4

Garlic heaven! In Crete, this soup is made with gigantes, the local dried butter beans which are the size of a small thumb, but split peas cook down in half the time and their flavour and the final texture of the soup is very similar. The salata, a miniature version of the ubiquitous Greek salad with all the ingredients finely diced, brings brightness and sparkle to the soup, while the burst of fresh garlic from the skordalia, a glorious traditional Greek sauce, is enough to scare off several nests of vampires.

Ingredients

4 tbsp and 150ml olive oil
450g onions, peeled and coarsely chopped
500g yellow split peas, rinsed
1 bay leaf
1 bushy rosemary sprig
1 tbsp bouillon powder
200g potatoes, peeled and cut into 2cm chunks
3 garlic cloves, peeled and crushed
50g blanched almonds
2 tbsp fresh lemon juice or white wine vinegar
4 tbsp water
100g cucumber, seeded and diced
200g plum cherry tomatoes, quartered
40g red onions, peeled and finely chopped
20 pitted black olives, halved
10g flat leaf parsley, coarsely chopped
10g fresh mint, coarsely chopped
1 tsp dried oregano
Sea salt and freshly ground black pepper

Tip: This is a filling, satisfying soup, yet energising and stimulating, a perfect lunch dish with a hunk of good, wholesome bread – but if you have an important date that evening, you might be wise to cook something less pungent!

Method

1 Heat 2 tbsp of oil in a large saucepan, add the onions and cook gently, stirring often, until soft and golden. Add the split peas, bay leaf and rosemary and pour in enough water to cover by 5cm. Bring to the boil, cover and simmer until the peas are totally soft, one and a half to two hours.

2 Cool slightly, remove the herbs, add the bouillon powder and some seasoning and blend in a food processor or with a hand-held electric blender until smooth. If it is very thick, add some water.

3 While the soup is cooking, make the skordalia by placing the potatoes in a small saucepan and covering with cold water. Bring to the boil, turn the heat right down and simmer until the potatoes are tender. Drain and cool for 10 minutes.

4 Blend the potatoes, 2 garlic cloves, almonds, lemon juice, water and some seasoning in a food processor until finely chopped and fairly smooth. With the motor running, slowly pour in 150ml of olive oil through the feeding tube. Check the seasoning and the acidity – it needs to have a good bite. If the skordalia is a bit solid, add some more water – you are looking for a creamy consistency so that it can be swirled into the soup.

5 For the Greek salata, place the remaining garlic clove, 2 tbsp of olive oil, cucumber, cherry tomatoes, red onions, olives and herbs in a bowl and mix gently. Add salt just before serving to ensure that the tomatoes do not go soggy.

6 Check the seasoning in the soup and ladle it into four warmed bowls; swirl in a couple of spoonfuls of skordalia, and top with a good dollop of Greek Salata.

7 Serve immediately and offer the remaining salata and skordalia separately.

Ribollita

Serves 4 generously

This classic Italian soup requires a bit of forward planning as dried beans work far better than the tinned variety: during their long cooking, they release their flavour and velvety starch into the stock, giving it both depth and body – but they need to be soaked overnight or given a lengthy cook, so either get yourself organised the day before, or give yourself plenty of time! The vegetables can be varied if desired – I have made it successfully with various root vegetables, but always include sturdy green leaves of some sort (cavolo nero if you can find it and want your soup to be authentically Tuscan, green cabbage, kale, or chard) as it would not be ribollita without it.

Tip: True Ribollita, meaning 'reboiled', is conventionally made with left-overs, but although it is a very good way of using up any cooked vegetables lurking in the refrigerator, the flavour is brighter and fresher if you cook it all from scratch.

Ingredients

200g pinto, cannellini or haricot beans, rinsed
3 tbsp olive oil plus extra to serve
450g onions, peeled and coarsely chopped
2 garlic cloves, peeled and thinly sliced
5 celery sticks, thinly sliced
275g carrots, scrubbed and diced
200g Savoy cabbage, thinly sliced
1 tbsp bouillon powder
2 sprigs of rosemary
2 bay leaves
1 x 400g tin chopped tomatoes
3 tbsp sun-dried tomato purée
4 thick slices wholemeal bread, roughly cut up into cubes
5g flat leaf parsley, coarsely chopped
Sea salt and freshly ground black pepper

Method

1 Place the beans in a medium saucepan, pour in enough cold water to cover them by 3cm, and bring to the boil.

2 Turn the heat right down, cover the saucepan and leave the beans to cook gently for a couple of hours, until really tender. Check them every now and then to make sure they are not drying out and, if necessary, add just enough water to keep them covered.

3 The beans keep for days in the refrigerator, so do prepare them ahead of time if that suits you.

4 When the beans are ready, mash them roughly with a potato masher or blitz them very briefly in a food processor – you need to keep some texture to them.

5 While the beans are cooking, heat 3 tbsp of olive oil in a large saucepan, stir in the onions and garlic, and cook gently, stirring occasionally, until soft and translucent, about 15 minutes.

6 Add the celery and carrots, cover the saucepan and cook for a further 15 minutes, again stirring occasionally. Add the cabbage, bouillon, herbs, tomatoes and purée, 500ml of water and some seasoning. Give it all a good stir, bring to the boil, cover the pan and simmer for one hour.

7 Add the beans and their cooking liquid, bring back to the boil and check the seasoning.

8 Divide the bread cubes between 4 warm soup bowls and ladle the soup over them.

9 Drizzle some olive oil over the top, sprinkle with parsley and serve immediately.

Griddled Courgette and Pepper Salad

Serves 4

Ensalada de calabacitas, or courgette salad, appears regularly on the menus of small provincial restaurants all over Mexico and varies from cook to cook. It always seems to feature courgettes and chillies, but many other ingredients are often included: sweetcorn, roasted peppers, toasted almonds or pumpkin seeds, and tomatoes are all frequent additions. 'Rajas', meaning strips or slices, are a traditional Mexican vegetable dish of green poblano chillies which are roasted or grilled, peeled and cut into strips. I tend to substitute red or yellow peppers for poblanos in a lot of Mexican dishes as I find that their sweetness and depth of flavour contribute a warm mellowness.

Ingredients

450g courgettes, washed
1 tsp and 4 tbsp olive oil and extra for brushing
50g pumpkin seeds
1 large red pepper and 1 large yellow or orange pepper, about 250g each, grilled
50g red onions, peeled and finely chopped
1 garlic clove, peeled and crushed
1 red chilli, deseeded and finely sliced
1 x 400g tin black or red kidney beans, rinsed and well drained
1 tsp dried Mexican or Greek oregano (see tip)
1 tbsp pumpkin seed butter (optional)
1 large lemon, zest and juice
10g fresh coriander, coarsely chopped
1/2 tsp chipotle chilli powder or to taste (see tip on page 29)
Sea salt and freshly ground black pepper

Tip: Mexican oregano is in fact not an oregano at all, but a member of the verbena family, while Greek oregano belongs among the mints. The Mexican variety is more pungent, less sweet, spicier and grassier. It is available by mail order. In the absence of Mexican oregano, do not hesitate to use the more common Greek one.

Method

1 Heat a ridged griddle pan over medium heat. Top and tail the courgettes and cut them lengthways into slices about 2mm thick. Discard the end slices which are all skin. Brush with olive oil and griddle on both sides until the courgettes start to soften and have acquired lovely golden stripes from the ridges. Place in a roomy salad bowl.

2 Mix the pumpkin seeds with 1 tsp of olive oil and some salt in a small frying pan and cook over low heat, stirring frequently, until they are nutty and just starting to brown. Set aside.

3 Skin the peppers and cut the flesh into 2cm pieces. Add to the salad bowl, along with the onions, garlic, chilli, beans, oregano, pumpkin seed butter, lemon zest and juice, and 4 tbsp of olive oil. Season and mix very gently. Set aside for about 30 minutes to allow the flavours to blend.

4 Add the pumpkin seeds to the salad and sprinkle first with coriander and then chipotle chilli powder.

5 Serve immediately.

La Socca

Serves 2 for lunch with a salad

The Niçoise socca, a pancake made from chickpea flour, is street food at its best – warm, fragrant, herby, crisp around the edges, soft in the middle. It is made in great big iron pans and the cook tears away slices with an enormous spatula before handing it to you in a piece of greaseproof paper. It is fabulous on its own, or it can be drizzled with tapenade, aïoli or rouille, whatever is on offer at the stall. It is simple, pretty much foolproof to make, both in a frying pan or in a roasting tin in the oven, and although the batter has to rest for an hour, there is virtually no preparation involved.

Ingredients

150g chickpea flour (see tip)
1 tsp fine sea salt
375ml water
2 tbsp finely chopped parsley, chives, rosemary or thyme
4 tbsp olive oil
2 x heavy non-stick frying pans, about 25cm in diameter

For the olive salsa:
25g red onions, peeled and finely chopped
1 garlic clove, peeled and crushed
15 black olives, stoned and coarsely chopped
5g flat leaf parsley, coarsely chopped
2 tbsp olive oil
1 lemon, grated zest and juice
Freshly ground black pepper

For the tomato salsa:
25g red onions, peeled and finely chopped
1 garlic clove, peeled and crushed
150g cherry tomatoes, quartered
2 tbsp sun-dried tomato purée
2 tbsp capers, rinsed and squeezed dry
5g fresh basil, shredded
Sea salt and freshly ground black pepper

Tip: Chickpea flour is also known as gram flour or besan. It is widely used in Indian recipes and makes a regular appearance in Mediterranean and Middle Eastern cuisine. It is gluten-free and incredibly useful in vegan cookery as it can take the place of eggs as a binding agent. It can be found in health shops and in the world food and baking sections of most large supermarkets.

Method

1 Place the chickpea flour, salt, water and herbs in a mixing bowl and whisk with an electric beater to make a smooth batter. Set aside to rest for an hour.

2 Make the olive salsa by mixing the onions, garlic, olives, parsley, olive oil, lemon zest, 1/2 tbsp of fresh lemon juice and some black pepper in a small bowl. Taste and add more lemon juice if it is a bit bland – it all depends on how briny the olives are.

3 Mix all the ingredients for the tomato salsa in a small bowl.

4 Heat the two frying pans over medium heat until the heat radiates from them.

5 Pour 2 tbsp of olive oil into each one and divide the batter between them. Lower the heat and leave the pancakes to cook until the edges start to brown – this will take three to four minutes. Flip them over with a wide spatula and cook the underside for about two minutes.

6 Slide the socca on to two warm plates and serve immediately with the salsas.

Black Bean Tostadas with Mango and Pomegranate Salsa

Makes 4 tostadas

'Tostar' means to toast, and tostadas are a popular Mexican street snack, consisting of a corn tortilla which is 'toasted' until it becomes golden, crisp and sturdy enough to support a spicy, savoury topping. While nowadays the tortilla is actually fried, in pre-Hispanic times, before cooking in fat became a traditional method in Mexican food preparation, it is likely that the tortilla was merely toasted on a dry griddle until it dried out and hardened. Tostada shells are available in packets in most supermarkets, but my much healthier version can easily be made at home in the oven.

Ingredients

250g black beans, rinsed
1 bay leaf
5 tbsp olive oil and extra for the tortillas
125g onions, peeled and coarsely chopped
2 garlic cloves, peeled and crushed
1 red chilli, deseeded and finely sliced
1 heaped tsp cumin seeds, toasted and medium ground (page 86)
4 x 15cm corn tortillas (page 146)
Seeds from 1/2 a large pomegranate (see tip)
1 small mango, peeled and diced
1 green chilli, deseeded and finely sliced
40g red onions, peeled and finely chopped
1 lime, juiced
15g fresh mint, coarsely chopped
250ml plain soya yoghurt, well seasoned (page 52)
Sea salt and freshly ground black pepper

Tip: Pomegranates are seasonal and widely available during the winter. The easiest way to remove the seeds is to roll it around on the work surface firmly with the heel of your hand before cutting into quarters - the seeds should then drop out without too much persuasion, but make sure you do not include any of the bitter white pith.

Method

1. Place the beans in a large saucepan with the bay leaf, add enough water to cover by 10cm and bring to the boil over medium heat. Turn the heat down to low, cover the saucepan and simmer very gently for at least two hours, until the beans are totally tender. Check them every now and then to make sure that they are not drying out and are covered by at least 1cm of water.

2. While the beans are cooking, heat 2 tbsp of olive oil in a heavy frying pan, add the onions, one garlic clove and the red chilli and cook over medium heat, stirring occasionally, until the onions are soft and starting to brown. Stir in the cumin and cook for a further minute.

3. To make the tostadas, preheat the oven to 160°C/325°F/Gas Mark 3/fan oven 140°C. Brush both sides of each tortilla lightly with olive oil, lay them out flat on a baking tray and cook in the oven for about 15 minutes, until they are crisp and starting to brown. Set aside to cool.

4. For the salsa, gently mix 3 tbsp of olive oil, pomegranate seeds, mango, green chilli, red onions, lime juice and mint together in a bowl.

5. When the beans are ready, transfer them to the frying pan with the onions using a slotted spoon and leaving most of the cooking liquid behind in the saucepan. Add some seasoning and mash the beans coarsely with a potato masher.

6. If the mixture is a bit thick and dry, add some of the cooking liquid – just enough to have a soft rather than stiff purée.

7. To serve, place the tostadas, beans, salsa and yoghurt on the table. Spread each tostada with beans, top with salsa and drizzle with yoghurt.

8. Eat immediately, before the tostadas go soggy and collapse!

Tip: Pomegranate juice has a horrible habit of staining both skin and fingernails so wear disposable gloves, which are cheap and easily available from supermarkets and chemists.

Butter Bean Ramen

Serves 4

Tip: Nori is a Japanese sea vegetable which comes in flakes or sheets which are most commonly used for wrapping sushi. It is high in vitamins and minerals and has a delicate but savoury flavour. Clearspring is a good brand and available in many large supermarkets or by mail order.

Ramen is a popular Japanese dish. At its simplest, it is just noodles in a well-flavoured broth, but more often than not it also contains diced vegetables, fish, strips of meat, and even seaweed. It is savoury and deeply comforting, ideal for a cold winter's night, and beautifully light as it is relatively fat-free. It is however very messy to eat, so be sure to provide a knife and fork as well as a spoon.

Ingredients

2 tbsp toasted sesame oil
200g red onions, peeled and coarsely chopped
1 red chilli, deseeded and finely sliced
2 garlic cloves, peeled and sliced
25g fresh ginger, peeled and finely chopped
200g shiitake or chestnut mushrooms, cleaned and quartered
1000ml vegetable stock, or water with 1 heaped tbsp bouillon powder
125g carrots, peeled and cut into strips
2 tbsp shoyu or tamari soy sauce (page 52)
250g Japanese noodles such as soba or udon (page 172)
2 x 400g butter beans, rinsed and drained
75g mangetouts, trimmed and strings removed
1 tbsp red or brown miso (page 52)
1 tbsp nori seaweed flakes (see tip)
2 fat spring onions, trimmed and finely sliced
10g fresh coriander, coarsely chopped
Sea salt and freshly ground black pepper

Method

1   Heat 1 tbsp of sesame oil in a medium saucepan and add the onions, chilli, garlic and ginger. Cook gently, stirring occasionally, until the onions turn translucent.

2   Stir in the mushrooms and continue to cook until they have released their moisture and are sizzling.

3   Pour in the stock and bring to the boil. Add the carrots and soy sauce, turn the heat right down, cover and leave to simmer until the carrots are tender, about 15 minutes.

4   Bring a large pot of salted water to the boil and cook the noodles according to the instructions on the packet. Drain well, return to the saucepan and stir in the remaining sesame oil. Keep warm.

5   Bring the broth back to the boil, add the butter beans and mangetouts and cook for one minute. Remove from the heat and stir in the miso, nori and some pepper.

6   Taste the broth and add a bit of salt if necessary – soy sauce, miso and seaweed are all salty so you may not need any salt at all. Stir in the spring onions and coriander.

7   Divide the noodles between 4 warm soup bowls and ladle the broth and vegetables over them.

8   Serve immediately.

North African Bean Salad In Pitta Pockets

Serves 2 as a lunch dish, 4 as a salad

The ports of France, not only in the Mediterranean but also the Atlantic coast, are one of the best places to experience authentic North African food in Europe. Immigrants from the old French colonies such as Algeria, Morocco and Tunisia have established restaurants catering not so much to the tourist trade or the French, but to their own local communities and visiting seafarers. I have often found that I end up eating in these restaurants rather than real French ones whenever I cross the Channel. I came across a version of this recipe in an Algerian restaurant in Cherbourg during a sailing holiday some years ago: a plate of plain couscous, the warm beans and a bowl of chermoula to drizzle over everything. I have refined and prettied it up slightly, but the original basic flavours have not changed.

Tip: Have plenty of paper napkins handy as the dressing tends to ooze out and make everything a bit messy!

Ingredients

150g thin French beans, top, tailed and halved
10g fresh mint
10g fresh coriander
1 heaped tsp cumin seeds, toasted and finely ground (page 86)
1/2 tsp sweet paprika
1/4 tsp saffron threads
120ml olive oil
1 small lemon, juiced
1 garlic clove, peeled
1 x 400g tin butter beans, rinsed and drained
25g raisins, plumped in hot water for 30 minutes and squeezed dry
25g pine nuts, toasted (page 86)
20 pitted black olives, halved
50g red onions, peeled and thinly sliced
125g cherry tomatoes, quartered
Large pitta breads, halved, to serve
Sea salt and freshly ground black pepper

Method

1 Cook the French beans in plenty of boiling, salted water for about three minutes – they need to have a bit of crispness to them. Drain, refresh in cold water and drain again. Place in a clean tea towel to dry out.

2 Make the dressing by blending the herbs, spices, olive oil, 1 tbsp of lemon juice, garlic and some seasoning until smooth. Taste and add a bit more lemon juice if it is all a bit flat – it should have a nice sharp edge.

3 In a roomy salad bowl, gently mix the green beans, butter beans, raisins, pine nuts, olives, red onions and cherry tomatoes. Season lightly.

4 Stir in the dressing and check the seasoning.

5 Fill the pitta breads with the bean salad.

6 Serve immediately before the bread goes soggy.

Spicy Lemony Lentils

Serves 2

Tip: Tan-coloured dried borlotti beans are just as delicious as the Puy lentils in this dish, and of course if you can find fresh borlotti in their magenta and cream pods during their brief season, pounce on them, they are gorgeous!

Lentils benefit from bold seasoning and partners. While they do have their own individual flavours, their main charm, in my opinion, is their texture and the way they absorb the essence and aromas of whatever else they are cooked with – be it a simple slick of extra virgin olive oil, or the punch of garlic, red onions, chilli and spices, brash gutsy herbs like basil and rosemary, and oranges and lemons. In this recipe, I am using the beautiful slate-green Puy lentils which boast their own Appellation Contrôlée; while their outstanding colour turns a bit sludgy in the saucepan, they hold their shape perfectly when cooked and retain their strangely pebbly texture even when lovely and soft.

Ingredients

175g Puy lentils, rinsed
1 large red and 1 large yellow pepper, about 250g each, grilled
50g red onions, peeled and finely chopped
1 garlic clove, peeled and crushed
1 hottish red chilli, deseeded and finely sliced
50g ready to eat dried apricots, diced
1 tsp sweet smoked paprika (pimentón dulce) or to taste (page 40)
3 pieces of prepared pickled lemon (page 25)
1 tbsp fresh lemon juice
5 tbsp olive oil
75g roasted salted almonds
25g flat leaf parsley, coarsely chopped
Sea salt and freshly ground black pepper

Method

1 Place the lentils in a saucepan and add enough cold water to cover by 5cm. Bring to the boil, cover the pan and leave to simmer until soft, about 40 minutes.

2 Skin the peppers and cut the flesh into 1cm wide strips. Place in a bowl and add the onions, garlic, chilli, apricots, paprika, pickled lemons, lemon juice and olive oil.

3 Drain the lentils well and gently stir them into the peppers, along with the almonds and parsley. Check the seasoning, heat and acidity, adding a bit more lemon juice and paprika if it all tastes a bit flat.

4 Divide the lentils between two warm plates and serve immediately.

Roasted Garlic and Borlotti Bean Purée

Serves 2

This purée takes time so save it for a day when you are very much in the mood for food! Smashing and peeling the garlic is somewhat labour intensive, and a rather sticky business, but if you are a garlic lover, you will feel that it was worth it. Borlotti beans make a wonderfully velvety purée, as the olive oil gives it all an unctuous richness, while the garlic makes for a tremendous depth of flavour which is absolutely addictive – you will find yourself thinking you have made enough purée for six people, only to find that you have gobbled up the whole lot between two of you. I tend to eat it on its own, with nothing more than some warm pitta bread, to really appreciate the unadulterated, pure garlickiness.

Ingredients

225g borlotti or pinto beans, rinsed
30 fat garlic cloves, smashed and peeled
2 tbsp and 100ml olive oil
Fresh lemon juice
Warm pitta bread, to serve (optional)
Sea salt and freshly ground black pepper

Method

1 Place the beans in a saucepan, add enough water to cover by 5cm and bring to the boil. Turn the heat right down, cover the pan and leave to cook until totally tender, about two hours.

2 Preheat the oven to 200°C/400°F/Gas Mark 6/fan oven 180°C.

3 Place the garlic in a small baking dish, drizzle with 2 tbsp of olive oil, wrap tightly in foil and bake for one hour, until soft.

4 With a slotted spoon, transfer the beans to the bowl of a food processor and add the garlic and its oil, the remaining olive oil, 1 tbsp of fresh lemon juice, some seasoning and just enough to the bean cooking liquid to help the blades turn effectively.

5 Process until smooth and check the seasoning, adding a bit more lemon juice if it needs some punch.

6 Return to the saucepan and reheat gently, stirring frequently.

7 Serve with warm pitta bread.

Tip: The easiest way to peel a clove of garlic is to give it a good whack with something solid like a rolling pin, jar of honey or tin of tomatoes. However, this obviously does not work if the cloves need to remain whole!

Felafel with Roasted Vegetables

Makes 8 felafel

The Middle East is littered with recipes for felafel but they seem to have originated in Egypt where they were, and still are, made from raw fresh or dried broad beans rather than the more common chickpeas. The beans are soaked with bicarbonate of soda and then ground with onions and spices, reminiscent of the Mauritian gâteau piment on page 198. This traditional method does however produce a rather dry and grainy felafel, so I tend to opt for cooked beans which give a softer, more moist result, and more often than not chickpeas instead of broad beans, as they come in a tin and make my life so much easier!

Tip: In this recipe, I have moved away from the normal salady and tzaziki-style accompaniments and partnered my felafel with savoury, caramelised roasted vegetables and a rich, sharp, sesame-based sauce. I prefer to shallow fry them in olive oil, although deep frying is a more authentic cooking method - but you do have to handle and turn them carefully as they are delicate.

Ingredients

For the felafel:
2 x 400g tins chickpeas, drained and well rinsed
3 garlic cloves, peeled
100g red onions, peeled and coarsely chopped
3 tbsp light tahini (page 109)
1/2 tsp ground turmeric
1 tbsp each cumin and coriander seeds, toasted and finely ground
2 1/2 tsp sea salt
Freshly ground black pepper
15g parsley, coarsely chopped
Wholemeal flour for dusting
Olive oil for frying

For the roasted vegetables:
6 tbsp olive oil
500g aubergines, peeled and cut into 2cm pieces
1 large red and 1 large yellow pepper, about 250g each, deseeded and cut into 2cm pieces
250g onions, peeled and sliced
2 garlic cloves, peeled and crushed
Sea salt and freshly ground black pepper

For the lemon tahini sauce:
250ml plain soya yoghurt
1 garlic clove, crushed
2 tbsp dark tahini (page 109)
2 tbsp toasted sesame or olive oil
Fresh lemon juice
Sea salt and freshly ground black pepper

Method

1 In a food processor, blend all the ingredients for the felafel, except the parsley, until relatively smooth – you don't want it to be velvety but largish pieces of chickpea tend to give it all a rather chalky texture. Add the parsley and blitz for a few seconds, just to mix it in properly. Scrape into a bowl and chill for 30 minutes.

2 With wet hands, shape the mixture into cakes about 5cm in diameter and 1.5cm high – a 5cm pastry ring is ideal for this but not essential. Place the felafel on a plate or baking tray and refrigerate again, for anything from one hour up to overnight.

3 Preheat the oven to 200°C/400F/Gas Mark 6/fan oven 180°C. Place all the ingredients for the roasted vegetables in a roasting tin, mix well, and roast, stirring occasionally, for about 45 minutes, until the aubergines are soft and golden, and the peppers and onions are starting to blacken along the edges. The vegetables can be prepared up to 24 hours ahead of time and reheated.

4 For the sauce, whisk the first four ingredients together with 1 tbsp of fresh lemon juice and some seasoning until smooth. Taste and add more lemon juice if it is not sharp enough – it all depends on the acidity of the yoghurt. Set aside until ready to use. The sauce can be refrigerated but be sure to bring it back to room temperature before serving.

5 Dust the felafel lightly with flour and heat some olive oil in a non-stick frying pan until fairly hot. Cook the felafel over medium heat for 4 to 5 minutes on each side, until crusty and golden.

6 Serve immediately with the roasted vegetables and sauce.

Tip: A certain
amount of
planning is
obviously
needed with
this recipe
as the beans
take at least a
good couple
of hours to
stew to the
required
luscious
softness, but
once they
have come to
the boil, they
can be left to
simmer on a
back burner;
and of course
if you cook
them the day
before, they
will be ready
to go and can
be turned
into delicious
chilaquiles
with little fuss
and effort.

Black Bean Chilaquiles with Cherry Tomato Salsa

Serves 4

Chilaquiles are the most Mexican of dishes, drawn from poverty cooking: a handful of stale tortillas moistened with a bit of sauce, normally tomato or bean. They are served mainly at breakfast and can be embellished with all sorts of extra ingredients, including salsas and grilled vegetables. The variations are endless and they are delicious in all their forms, from the simplest and most basic to the fanciest versions served in expensive restaurants.

Ingredients

500g black beans, rinsed
200g onions, peeled and finely sliced
3 garlic cloves, peeled and crushed
1 bay leaf
1 tbsp chipotle chilli paste (page 29)
2 tbsp olive oil
250g plain tortilla chips
1 x Basic Cherry Tomato Salsa, made with fresh coriander (page 23)
250ml plain soya yoghurt, well seasoned (page 52)
Sea salt and freshly ground black pepper

Method

1 Place the beans in a large saucepan with the onions, garlic cloves and bay leaf, add enough water to cover by 10cm, and bring to the boil over medium heat. Turn the heat down to low, cover the saucepan and simmer very gently for at least two hours, preferably three or four, until the beans are totally tender. Check them every now and then to make sure that they are not drying out and are covered by at least 1cm of water. Add some seasoning and cook for another 20 minutes.

2 Drain the beans, reserving the cooking liquid and discarding the bay leaf. Place them in a large, deep frying pan or wok and heat them gently, mashing them with a potato masher to a coarse purée. Stir in the chipotle chilli paste, olive oil and just enough of the cooking liquid to bring the beans to a soupy consistency.

3 Add the tortilla chips and turn them over and over in the bean purée with a large spoon until they are well coated and start to soften. Check the seasoning.

4 Transfer to a large, deep serving dish, drizzle with yoghurt and spoon the salsa over the top.

5 Serve immediately.

Jewelled Wild Rice Salad

Serves 2 as a main course, 4 as a side dish

'Wild' rice's days in the wilderness are over and it has become very tame. It started off as a grass in North America, growing in the shallow waters of small lakes and streams but increased demand led to commercial cultivation in paddy fields. It requires fairly extensive cooking, a good 50 minutes at least, to burst the dark outer casing and soften the interior, and however long you cook it, it always provides good exercise for the jaw muscles. However, this chewy texture is one of its charms, as are its nutty flavour and dramatic colour.

Ingredients

120g wild rice
Seeds from 1 small pomegranate (see tip on page 62)
2 small oranges, peeled, segmented and juice reserved
25g red onions, peeled and finely sliced
1 hottish red chilli, deseeded and finely sliced
1 tbsp capers, rinsed and squeezed dry, chopped if large
2 tbsp pomegranate molasses (see tip)
25g shelled pistachios, toasted
3 tbsp olive oil
10g fresh coriander, coarsely chopped
Sea salt and freshly ground black pepper

**Tip:
Pomegranate molasses, with its sweet and sour fruitiness and deep caramel tones, is available from delicatessens, some supermarkets and by mail order.**

Method

1 Cook the rice according to the packet instructions and drain well.

2 Place the pomegranate seeds in a roomy salad bowl with the oranges and their juice. Gently stir in the rice, some salt and pepper, and all the remaining ingredients.

3 Check the seasoning and serve.

Kedgeree

Serves 4

Kedgeree has undergone many transformations, and although there are claims that it originated in Scotland, it is more likely that it started off in India as kichri, a simple dish of rice and lentils flavoured with spices. The British upgraded it with the addition of fish and hard-boiled eggs and it took pride of place at the Victorian breakfast table. In this recipe, I am returning to its Indian – and vegan – roots and flavouring it with chillies and ginger. I always think of kedgeree as a soothing dish and have therefore used just one red chilli and korma curry paste; if, however, you like it hot, feel free to add more chillies and use a Madras or Vindaloo paste.

Tip: All the different elements of the kedgeree - rice, lentils and carrots, and onion mixture, can be prepared ahead of time, leaving you with nothing more to do than heat it all up together.

Ingredients

2 tbsp coconut or olive oil (page 164)
150g brown basmati rice
1/2 tsp ground turmeric
1 tbsp green cardamom pods
1 cinnamon stick
1 tsp bouillon powder
400ml boiling water
75g brown lentils, rinsed
175g carrots, scrubbed and diced
250g onions, peeled and coarsely chopped
25g ginger, peeled and finely chopped
2 garlic cloves, peeled and crushed
40g raisins
1 large red chilli, deseeded and finely sliced
4 tbsp korma curry paste
1 tbsp garam masala
100g frozen petits pois, defrosted
100g roasted, salted cashews, coarsely chopped
10g flat leaf parsley, coarsely chopped
Sea salt and freshly ground black pepper

Method

1. Heat 1 tbsp of oil in a medium saucepan, add the rice, spices and bouillon, and stir-fry for a minute. Pour in the boiling water, cover the pan, turn the heat right down, and cook for 50 minutes.

2. Stir the rice gently with a skewer and set aside to cool.

3. Place the lentils and carrots in a small pan, add enough water to cover by 5cm and cook for about 40 minutes, until tender. Drain.

4. While the rice and lentils are cooking, heat the remaining oil in a wide, deep frying pan, add the onions, ginger and garlic, and cook gently, stirring often, until it all starts to brown, about 15 minutes.

5. Add the raisins, chilli and some seasoning, and cook for a further 10 minutes.

6. Stir in the curry paste and garam masala, and fry for a minute or two before turning the heat up to medium and adding the rice and lentils.

7. Turn it all over and over in the onion mixture with a large spoon so that the rice absorbs the flavours while it heats.

8. When everything is nice and steaming, lightly fold in the petits pois, cashews and parsley and check the seasoning.

9. Serve immediately.

French Bean and Sweetcorn Salad

Serves 2

Pumpkin seeds, lightly toasted in oil and well salted, are a favourite Mexican street snack, sold on the street corners in paper cornets or even just a twist of the day's newspaper. They are packed with protein and essential fatty acids, but their real beauty is their haunting flavour, more than nutty, more than rich, faintly green and grassy. Their oil is quite sublime, and if you fancy investing in a bottle of this green gold, do use it for the dressing. Pumpkins, beans, tomatoes and sweetcorn all originated in the Americas, and I have added a chopped fresh chilli to give the salad a Mexican twist.

Tip: If you don't have any French beans, frozen peas are also delicious in this salad. Defrost them completely and dry them out slightly in a tea towel as described.

Ingredients

20g pumpkin seeds
1 tsp and 4 tbsp olive oil
100g French beans, topped, tailed and halved
200g tinned or frozen sweetcorn, rinsed and well drained
100g cherry tomatoes, quartered
1 garlic clove, peeled and crushed
50g red onions, peeled and thinly sliced
1 red chilli, deseeded and finely sliced
15g chives, finely snipped with scissors
Sea salt and freshly ground black pepper

Method

1 Preheat the oven to 160°C/325°F/Gas Mark 3/fan oven 145°C. Spread the pumpkin seeds in a small baking dish, stir in 1 tsp of olive oil, sprinkle with salt and bake for about 20 minutes, stirring occasionally, until the seeds start to turn a light gold and smell nice and toasty. Set aside to cool.

2 Bring a large pan of salted water to the boil and cook the French beans for about 3 minutes, until tender and crisp. Drain and refresh in cold water. Drain again, shaking out any remaining moisture. Wrap them in a clean tea towel to dry them out totally.

3 Mix all the ingredients together in a salad bowl with some seasoning and serve immediately.

Rice in the Style of Veracruz

Serves 4

Veracruz in the Gulf of Mexico was the most important port in New Spain during the colonial period and today it lies at the centre of the import/export trade with the United States, Latin America and Europe, which has turned it into a vast melting pot of culinary influences. There was no rice in Mexico until after the Spanish conquest and this dish of rice flavoured with tomatoes is an excellent example of the fusion of Old and New World ingredients in Mexican cuisine. The final texture is moist and quite soft, rather like a risotto.

Tip: Basmati rice has a wonderfully nutty flavour and its grains cook to a fluffy consistency which works well in pilaus and 'stewed' dishes like this one.

Ingredients

400g tomatoes
2 tbsp olive oil
125g onions, peeled and coarsely chopped
1 garlic clove, peeled and finely sliced
1 hot red chilli, deseeded and finely sliced
2 bay leaves
150g carrots, scrubbed and diced
150g brown basmati rice
1 tsp bouillon powder
1 tsp salt
400ml boiling water
125g frozen petits pois, defrosted

Method

1   Purée the tomatoes in a blender or food processor until smooth.

2   Heat the olive oil in a medium saucepan, add the onions, garlic and chilli and cook gently, stirring occasionally, until soft and just starting to brown.

3   Stir in the bay leaves, carrots and rice and cook for a further five minutes.

4   Add the bouillon, salt and tomato purée, and pour in the boiling water. Give it all a good stir, bring back to the boil and turn the heat right down. Cover the pan and cook undisturbed for 50 minutes to one hour, until the rice is tender and has absorbed all the liquid.

5   Remove from the heat and add the petits pois.

6   Stir the rice gently with a skewer, cover the pan again and leave to rest for 10 minutes.

7   Stir once more with the skewer and serve immediately.

Polenta with Sweetcorn, Roasted Tomatoes, Olives and Capers

Serves 4

Polenta is simply cornmeal and true peasant food from Northern Italy. It can be served 'wet' as in this recipe, soft and tender, reminiscent of a cooked breakfast cereal; or it can be spread out on a baking tray, left to cool, cut into squares or rounds and fried, thereby acquiring a golden crust to contrast with the soft interior.

Tip: Polenta goes very solid soon after being taken off the heat so it is important not to leave it sitting around once it is ready or you will find yourself eating concrete!

Ingredients

250g cherry tomatoes, halved

4 tbsp olive oil

275g red onions, peeled and coarsely chopped

500ml water

1 tbsp bouillon powder

1 tbsp Dijon mustard

125g polenta

25 pitted black olives, halved

2 tbsp capers, rinsed and squeezed dry

275g frozen or tinned sweetcorn, rinsed and well drained

10g basil, shredded

Sea salt and freshly ground black pepper

Method

1 Preheat the oven to 200°C/400°F/Gas Mark 6/fan oven 180°C.

2 Line a baking tray with baking parchment, arrange the tomatoes on it, cut side up, season them lightly and cook for about 45 minutes, until slightly shrivelled and charred around the edges.

3 Heat 2 tbsp of olive oil in a medium saucepan and fry the onions gently until soft and translucent, about 15 minutes.

4 Add the water, bouillon powder, mustard and some seasoning, and bring to the boil.

5 Place the polenta in a jug and pour it slowly into the boiling water in a steady stream, stirring all the time.

6 Turn the heat down as low as possible and cook the polenta according to the instructions on the packet until thick and smooth.

7　Add the olives, capers, sweetcorn and basil, and check the seasoning.

8　Carefully fold in the tomatoes and remaining olive oil and serve immediately.

Mexican Bean Dip

Serves 4

Pulses of all sorts are a staple ingredient in Mexican cooking, and chillies are used extensively not only to add heat and sparkle, but to enhance flavour. This dip, reminiscent of the ubiquitous refried beans, is seasoned with a powder of chipotle, the dried version of the well-known jalapeño chilli which is smoked, giving it a strong whiff of caramel.

Ingredients

2 x 400g tins red kidney beans, rinsed and drained
2 garlic cloves, peeled
50g red onions, peeled and coarsely chopped
1 tbsp cumin seeds, toasted and finely ground (page 86)
4 tbsp olive oil
2 tbsp dark tahini
1 tsp chipotle chilli powder
1 large lemon, grated zest and juice
10g fresh coriander
1 red chilli, deseeded and finely sliced
Sea salt
Tortilla chips, to serve

Method

1　Place the first eight ingredients in a food processor, season with salt, and process until fairly smooth.

2　Scrape into a bowl and garnish with coriander and red chilli.

3　Serve with tortilla chips.

Tip: The flavours in this dip tend to develop in intensity so if you are intending to make it several hours or even days ahead of time, recheck the seasoning before serving – if it is all a bit strong, add a couple of tablespoons of water to balance it.

Confetti Tabbouleh

Serves 4

Versions of this typically Lebanese salad are found all over the Middle East and North Africa and, like all traditional dishes, vary from country to country, region to region, family to family and cook to cook. However, there are four particular ingredients which are considered essential: bulgur wheat, parsley, mint and lemon. The proportions depend on the individual; I once watched Claudia Roden demonstrate the preparation of tabbouleh, and I remember her comment on this subject: 'Tabbouleh should be green with buff specks'. I personally prefer a higher proportion of the said buff specks, about half bulgur and half chopped herbs, along with some fruit for sweetness, some nuts for crunch and protein, and the sour, caramel notes of pomegranate molasses to bring it all together.

Ingredients

300ml water
1 tsp bouillon powder
1 large lemon, juiced
150g bulgur wheat
125g red cherry tomatoes, quartered
1 small, ripe mango, peeled and diced
100g frozen petits pois, defrosted
50g red onions, peeled and finely chopped
1 garlic clove, peeled and crushed
2 tbsp pomegranate molasses (see tip on page 73)
5 tbsp olive oil
10g flat leaf parsley, coarsely chopped
10g mint, coarsely chopped
50g toasted, slivered almonds
Sea salt and freshly ground black pepper

Tip: Bulgur wheat requires rehydrating in hot or cold water, depending on how you are serving it, and absorbs other flavours willingly, so I add bouillon powder and lemon juice at this stage, to give them a chance to permeate the salad. Look for wholegrain bulgur, as it is often debranned.

Method

1 Bring the water to the boil in a medium saucepan, stir in the bouillon, 2 tbsp of the lemon juice and 1 tsp of salt. Take the pan off the heat, pour in the bulgur, give it all a good stir and cover the pan.

2 Leave the bulgur to rehydrate for about 30 minutes or even overnight in the refrigerator if it suits you. Fluff it up with a fork and set it aside to cool while you prepare the other ingredients.

3 In a roomy salad bowl, combine the tomatoes, mango, petit pois, onions, garlic, molasses and olive oil.

4 Tip the bulgur into the bowl, grind in some black pepper, and stir it all gently with a fork. Check the seasoning, adding more lemon juice if it is not sharp enough.

5 Fold in the herbs and almonds and serve immediately.

Tip: Bulgur is wheat grains which have been parboiled and dried, which provides a wonderful earthiness and chewy texture.

Waldorf Salad Quinoa

Serves 2 as a main dish

Waldorf Salad was reputedly created in 1895, not by a chef but by the maître d'hôtel at the Waldorf Astoria Hotel in New York, where it promptly became a signature dish. It has undergone many transformations over the years, and its reputation was greatly enhanced by its appearance at the table in an episode of the television series, Fawlty Towers, in 1979. However, it remains a classic and wherever it is made, it is sure to contain the original apples and celery, as well as the later inclusion of walnuts. The addition of quinoa makes it into a satisfying main dish.

Tip: Quinoa was sacred to the Incas, who referred to it as 'the mother of all grains'. Unusually for a plant food, it is a complete protein containing all the essential amino acids, as well as being rich in minerals.

Ingredients

500ml water
1 tbsp bouillon powder
200g quinoa
1 large red apple, about 150g, cored and diced
2 celery sticks, finely sliced
4 spring onions, trimmed and finely sliced
2 to 3 tbsp fresh lemon juice
3 tbsp sesame, walnut or hazelnut oil
5g fresh sage, coarsely chopped
15g flat leaf parsley, coarsely chopped
100g walnut pieces, toasted (page 102)
Sea salt and freshly ground black pepper

Method

1 Bring the water to the boil in a medium saucepan, add the bouillon, quinoa and some pepper, and bring back to the boil.

2 Turn the heat down as low as possible, cover the saucepan and cook for 20 minutes.

3 Remove from the heat and fluff the quinoa up with a skewer.

4 Add the apple, celery, spring onions, 2 tbsp of lemon juice and the oil. Stir gently with the skewer and check the seasoning and acidity, adding a bit of salt and more lemon juice if necessary, as much depends on the sweetness of the apple. Fold in the herbs and walnuts.

5 Serve immediately.

Pugliese Split Pea Purée with Wilted Greens

Serves 4 as a supper dish with bread and a salad

Peasant food from the heel of Italy, which I discovered during a visit to Apulia many years ago, long before this southern province and its sun-dried tomatoes became fashionable and well known. The selection of vegetarian – and vegan – food in restaurants was extraordinary, perhaps evidence of the historical poverty of this part of the country. The purée is traditionally made with dried broad beans, and wild greens, specifically chicory – cicoria, but yellow split peas are more easily available, as are spinach and chard – unless of course you are a born forager!

Ingredients

500g yellow split peas, rinsed
1 bay leaf
375g onions, peeled and coarsely chopped
1 tbsp bouillon powder
300g baby spinach or chard, washed
120ml olive oil
2 garlic cloves, peeled and finely sliced
75g red onions, peeled and finely sliced
Sea salt and freshly ground black pepper

Tip: Never add salt to any kind of pulse until it is fully cooked, as seasoning in the early stages toughens the skins.

Method

1   Place the peas in a heavy saucepan, pour in enough fresh water to cover them by 3cm, add the bay leaf and onions, and bring to the boil over medium heat. Turn the heat right down, cover the pan and leave the peas to simmer gently until they are totally soft and you have a thick purée, about two hours. Stir in the bouillon powder and some seasoning.

2   If you are using chard, remove the thick ribs and slice the leaves across into ribbons about 1cm wide.

3   While the peas are cooking, heat half the olive oil in a large frying pan or wok, add the garlic and stir-fry it until golden – keep an eye on it as it burns easily and turns bitter.

4   A few minutes before you are ready to serve, toss the spinach or chard into the hot frying pan with the garlic and cook over high heat until wilted and soft. Season.

5   Ladle the purée into four warm bowls and drizzle the remaining olive oil over each portion. Spoon the garlicky spinach or chard on top and sprinkle with the sliced red onions.

6   Serve immediately.

5

Nuts, Seeds and Oils – Opulence and Intensity

Nuts and seeds are a valuable source of protein and healthy fats but their talents do not stop there. A short blast in the oven or a quick stir-fry in a little oil produce a magical result, bringing out their warm, rich flavour which manages to be both subtle and intense. A sprinkling of toasted almonds over a salad, some pine nuts in a dish of pasta or a handful of cashews in a curry for instance, lift the whole dish to a totally new level. They can be the principal player, as in the hazelnut soup on page 99 or the gianduia ice cream on page 112, or they can stay well in the background, adding a delicate note of luxury, perhaps a contrast of texture, and always a noticeable depth.

The high fat content in seeds and nuts makes them very perishable, as the oil can go rancid very quickly, so always buy them in sealed packets rather than loose – there is no way of knowing how long a nut has been hanging around in a health shop bin and how effectively the stock is rotated. Once the packet is opened, store any unused nuts and seeds in the freezer to ensure freshness.

Almost all nuts and seeds are available as 'butters', from the ubiquitous and fairly overpowering peanut butter and incredibly useful Middle Eastern sesame or tahini, to the more unusual and considerably more interesting pumpkin or sunflower seed butters – it is worth having a selection of these to hand as they make a quick and easy snack and can be used in salad dressings, soups, pastas, etc. They are available in health shops, some supermarkets and by mail order (page 16-17). Once the jar is opened, it is important to keep it in the refrigerator to prevent staleness and mould.

One invaluable role for seeds and nuts which I have discovered recently is in a vegan 'cheese' or 'mayonnaise'. I routinely made pestos and sauces, for instance, with tofu but now I soak nuts or seeds overnight, blend them until smooth, add herbs and flavourings like mustard and bouillon powder, and end up with a sort of 'cream cheese' mixture with a myriad of uses. Cashews and pine nuts work best here as their flavour is quite delicate; cashews are cheaper than pine nuts and are therefore usually my first choice; they do, however, have a sweet edge which is not always ideal.

Nuts and seeds, rich olives and unctuous avocadoes make wonderfully fragrant and aromatic oils, which are well worth the investment they often entail; and if you are stocking up on this kind of luxury, you may as well throw caution and budget to the winds and splurge on a bottle of haunting black truffle oil as well! While toasted sesame oil can be used in cooking, the more delicate oils like hazelnut, avocado, macadamia and pumpkin, let alone truffle, are best kept for dressings, sauces and drizzling. Needless to say, all oils should be cold-pressed and extra virgin, and refrigerated once opened.

How to toast nuts and seeds

Cooking nuts and seeds in the oven or in a frying pan until golden really brings out their rich, toasty flavour but be careful not to overcook them as they can go quite bitter.

Method

1 Preheat the oven to 160°C/325°F/Gas Mark 3/fan oven 145°C. Spread the nuts or seeds out on a baking tray and toast in the oven until lightly golden. The cooking time depends on the size: pine nuts, for instance, take about 10 minutes, while walnuts and pecans need about 20. The best way to tell whether they are ready is by the smell, which should be toasty and rich.

2 Cool before use.

Basic Nut Cheese or Mayonnaise

Pretty much all nuts and seeds can be used to make this 'cheese', although pine nuts and cashews tend to work better as their raw flavour is fairly mild. It is extremely versatile and makes a regular appearance in my vegan cooking. It is also an excellent building block for many vegan sauces. If you can remember to soak the nuts overnight in mineral or filtered water, you will have a much smoother cheese; drain and rinse the soaked nuts before use.

Ingredients

125g raw nuts
1 garlic clove, peeled
4 tbsp olive oil
4 tbsp water
1 tbsp smooth Dijon mustard
1 tbsp fresh lemon juice
1 tsp bouillon powder
Sea salt and freshly ground black pepper

Method

Blend all the ingredients together until smooth.

Aïoli

Pine nuts are the basis of this vegan version of the wonderfully garlicky Provençal sauce.

Ingredients

100g raw pine nuts
2 garlic cloves, peeled
3 tbsp plain soya yoghurt
1 tsp smooth Dijon mustard
120ml olive oil
Zest and juice of 1 small lemon
Sea salt and freshly ground black pepper

Method

Blend all the ingredients together until smooth. Add a bit of water if it is too thick.

Mustard Mayonnaise

All types of mustard work well in this recipe – Dijon, wholegrain, English, American, green peppercorn – but obviously some are stronger than others so start off with a tablespoon of whichever one you choose and work up from there.

Ingredients

125g raw cashew nuts
1 tbsp smooth Dijon mustard
1/2 tsp wholegrain mustard
1 tsp bouillon powder
1 garlic clove, peeled
3 tbsp olive oil
Fresh lemon juice
Sea salt and freshly ground black pepper

Method

Blend the nuts, mustards, bouillon powder, garlic, olive oil and 1 tbsp of lemon juice until smooth. Check the seasoning and add a bit more lemon juice if the flavour needs brightening.

Rouille

This very typical Provençal mayonnaise is flavoured with grilled red peppers, paprika and plenty of garlic. Freshly grilled peppers, prepared at home, are obviously best but I have been known to use a jar of roasted peppers when I have needed to cut corners!

Ingredients

1 large red pepper, about 250g, grilled
100g raw cashew nuts
2 garlic cloves, peeled
8 tbsp olive oil
1 tsp hot or sweet smoked paprika (pimentón picante or dulce) (see tip on page 128)
2 tsp smooth Dijon mustard
1 tbsp fresh lemon juice
Sea salt and freshly ground black pepper

Method

1   Skin the pepper and dice the flesh.

2   Place in a blender or food processor with all the remaining ingredients and blend until smooth.

3   Check the seasoning.

Bean and Mushroom Soup with a Drizzle of Truffle Oil

Tip: The real investment when making this soup is the purchase of the truffle oil! Although small bottles are available at supermarkets and seem very affordable, their truffle content is minimal and they are a waste of money. So treat yourself to a large bottle with an Italian or French label, at a good delicatessen.

Serves 2 as a main course

Dried wild mushrooms are available all year and are an excellent kitchen standby, as their flavour is intense and woodsy, considerably stronger than their fresh wild counterparts, let alone any kind of domesticated mushroom. They can be expensive but a little goes a long way and just one small packet will add depth and body to anything from a soup to a sauce or a vegetable medley. They can be found in the fresh produce sections of most large supermarkets, as well as delicatessens.

Ingredients

25g dried porcini mushrooms
4 tbsp olive oil
200g onions, peeled and coarsely chopped
300ml medium dry cider
150ml sweet Marsala wine
2 x 400g tins butter beans, drained and rinsed
1 heaped tsp bouillon powder
400g button mushrooms, cleaned, stalks trimmed, and thickly sliced
10 sage leaves, finely chopped
Truffle oil (see tip)
Sea salt and freshly ground black pepper

Method

1 Place the porcini in a small bowl and cover with boiling water. Leave to rehydrate for 30 minutes and strain, reserving the soaking liquid.

2 Heat 2 tbsp of olive oil in a medium saucepan and add the onions. Cook gently, stirring often, until golden, about 20 minutes.

3 Pour in the cider and Marsala, and simmer until reduced to a couple of spoonfuls.

4 Stir in the beans, porcini, bouillon powder, some seasoning and enough water to cover by 1cm. Carefully add all but the last couple of spoonfuls of the porcini soaking liquid, which will be full of sediment.

5 Bring to the boil, cover and leave to cook gently for 20 minutes. Cool slightly and purée in a food processor. Return the soup to the saucepan, check the seasoning and reheat before serving.

6 While the soup is cooking, heat the remaining olive oil in a frying pan, add the mushrooms, sage and some seasoning, and cook, stirring occasionally, until they are nice and brown.

7 Ladle the soup into two warm soup bowls, divide the mushrooms between them and drizzle liberally with black truffle oil.

8 Serve immediately.

Tip: Keep your truffle oil in the fridge, and feast on it occasionally, indulging your taste buds and olfactory senses by swirling a generous spoonful of it into this soup for instance.

Middle Eastern Fig Salad

Serves 4

Revered by the early Hebrews as a reflection of peace and plenty, and one of the four historic Mediterranean foods, along with olives, grapes and wheat, figs are now relatively available all year round, but like strawberries and asparagus in mid-winter, they have little flavour or colour, their pale green skins are thick and coarse, their seedy hearts bland and anaemic. Nevertheless, sometime in August, big fat purple figs suddenly make a brief appearance, and this is the only time to eat them. They are bursting with juice and sunshine, honeyed and sweet, their skins taut and tinged with a delicate white bloom.

Tip: Do figs need to be peeled? I never do but there is a rather charming Italian proverb which admonishes you to feed the skin of a fig to your enemy and the skin of a peach to your friend.

Ingredients

50g skinned almonds
1 tsp and 6 tbsp olive oil
1/8 tsp chilli powder
1/4 tsp salt
50g rocket
4 ripe purple figs, quartered
2 pieces of prepared pickled lemon (page 25)
1 tsp red wine vinegar
10g fresh mint, coarsely chopped
2 spring onions, trimmed and finely sliced
Freshly ground black pepper

Method

1   Preheat the oven to 160°C/326°F/Gas Mark 3/fan oven 145°C.

2   Place the almonds in a small baking dish and add 1 tsp of olive oil, the chilli powder and salt. Stir it all well together to coat the almonds. Bake in the oven for 20 to 30 minutes, until golden and aromatic. Allow to cool.

3   Arrange the rocket on two plates and place the fig quarters on top.

4   In a small bowl or ramekin, mix together the pickled lemon, vinegar, mint, spring onions, remaining olive oil and some seasoning. Pour the dressing over the salad.

5   Top with almonds and serve immediately.

need2know

Muhammara Salad

Serves 2 as a light lunch

Muhammara is reputedly a speciality of Aleppo in Syria, a dip rather than a salad, rich with walnuts, fragrant with mint, spiked with cumin and, when I make it, the smoky, aromatic heat of pimentón, the smoked paprika so popular in Spanish cooking – so this is obviously not an authentic muhammara but, as you will see, the pimentón adds very considerably to the flavour and interest.

Ingredients

4 large red peppers, about 250g each, grilled
2 garlic cloves, peeled
80g wholemeal bread
125ml and 2 tbsp olive oil
1/2 tsp sweet or hot smoked paprika (pimentón dulce or picante) or to taste (page 128)
2 tsp cumin seeds, toasted and coarsely ground
100g walnuts, toasted
Fresh lemon juice
20 pitted black olives, halved
15g mint, coarsely chopped
Pitta bread, to serve (optional)
Sea salt and freshly ground black pepper

Tip: Breadsticks, any robust loaf, tortilla chips and crudités are all good accompaniments instead of pitta bread.

Method

1   Skin the peppers and discard the seeds and stalks. Place in a food processor with the garlic, bread, 125ml of olive oil, pimentón, cumin, walnuts, about 1 tbsp of lemon juice and some salt and pepper. Process to a smooth purée.

2   Check the seasoning and acidity, adding a bit more lemon juice if the flavour is at all flat.

3   Spread the muhammara out on a large, flat serving dish. Garnish with olives and mint, and drizzle with the remaining olive oil.

4   Serve immediately or cover with cling film until you are ready to eat.

Roasted Butternut Squash, Red Onion and Walnut Salad

Serves 4

Butternut squash, like pumpkins and their other relatives – which by the way include cucumbers and melons – are not bulging with culinary potential, but careful cooking and accurate partnering do bring out a certain amount of glamour. In spite of being a fruit rather than a vegetable and having a high sugar content, all squashes for me are a savoury food, which goes particularly well with nuts and bold flavours like onion, garlic and chilli.

Ingredients

1 butternut squash, about 1400g
4 tbsp olive oil
2 bushy rosemary sprigs
2 fresh bay leaves
250g red onions, peeled and sliced
8 very thin slices walnut bread
4 tbsp walnut or hazelnut oil
1 tbsp hazelnut butter (optional)
1 tsp balsamic vinegar
100g rocket, washed and dried
100g walnut pieces, toasted (page 86)
Sea salt and freshly ground black pepper

Method

1 Preheat the oven to 200°C/400°F/Gas Mark 6/fan oven 180°C.

2 Halve the squash, scrape out the seeds and any fibrous bits, peel and cut into 2cm chunks. Place in a roasting tray, season well, tuck in the rosemary and bay, and drizzle it all with the olive oil. Roast on the top shelf of the oven for 30 minutes.

3 Stir in the red onions and cook for a further half hour.

4 Brush the walnut bread on both sides with some of the walnut oil, lay the slices out on a foil-lined baking tray and put them on the middle shelf of the oven, below the squash, to crisp and brown for about 15 minutes, turning them over halfway through. Set aside until you are ready to serve.

Tip: Roasting pumpkin or squash in oil until it is lightly golden and caramelised is an essential step: the flesh is 90% water and unless you cook away all this moisture, you are left with a pretty colour but not much else. Roasting concentrates the flavour, firms the flesh, and turns a pumpkin from flabby to fabulous, from a rather plain stepsister into a bit of a belle.

5 Whisk the remaining walnut oil, the hazelnut butter and vinegar in a medium bowl with some seasoning to make a dressing. Add the rocket, toss gently and arrange on 4 plates.

6 Remove the herbs from the squash, stir in the toasted walnuts and spoon over the rocket.

7 Garnish with the walnut bread croûtons and serve immediately.

Croûtes Provençales with Aïoli

Makes 4 croûtes

This is a simplified version of a pizza, without the hassle of making dough or rolling pastry. Slices of bread are brushed with oil and topped with a rich, savoury tomato sauce before being baked in the oven. Aïoli, one of the most famous Provençal sauces, is a thick, glossy mayonnaise heavily laced with garlic, and this vegan version, based on a nut cheese, is just as robust and addictive.

Tip: The tomato sauce can be made ahead of time, but don't assemble the croûtes until you are ready to put them in the oven or they will go soggy.

Ingredients

3 tbsp olive oil
400g onions, peeled and sliced
3 garlic cloves, peeled and crushed
500g tomatoes, skinned and chopped
1 fresh bay leaf
4 thick slices wholemeal bread
15g capers, rinsed and squeezed dry
8 pitted black olives, halved
2 tbsp finely chopped parsley
1 x quantity aïoli, made with pine nuts
Sea salt and freshly ground black pepper

Method

1   Heat 2 tbsp of olive oil in a large frying pan and add the onions and crushed garlic. Cook gently, stirring occasionally, until soft and lightly golden.

2   Stir in the tomatoes, bay leaf and some seasoning, and continue to simmer, stirring occasionally and breaking the tomatoes down with the back of a spoon, until most of the excess moisture has evaporated and you have a thick, savoury sauce.

3   Preheat the oven to 200°C/400°F/Gas Mark 6/fan oven 180°C.

4   Brush both sides of the bread with the remaining olive oil and arrange on a baking tray lined with kitchen foil. Divide the tomato mixture between the four slices and top with the capers and olives.

5   Bake in the oven for 15 minutes.

6   Sprinkle the croûtes with parsley and serve immediately, with the aïoli on the side.

Roasted Mediterranean Vegetables with Rouille

Serves 4

Rouille is a spicy, bright orange mayonnaise from southern France which is typically served with the very Mediterranean fish soup. In this recipe, it melts down into the hot, caramelised vegetables, creating a dish full of sunshine and fragrance, while the roasted garlic cloves are soft, golden and utterly addictive.

Ingredients

550g aubergines, washed, peeled and cut into chunks
550g courgettes, washed and sliced into 1cm rounds
5 tbsp olive oil
400g red and/or yellow peppers, seeded and cut into 1cm wide slices
1 head of garlic, separated into cloves, unpeeled
250g baby plum tomatoes, halved
65g sunflower seeds
50g red onions, peeled and finely chopped
15g fresh basil, shredded
1 x quantity rouille (page 89)
Sea salt and freshly ground black pepper

Method

1   Preheat the oven to 200°C/400°F/Gas Mark 6/fan oven 180°C.

2   Place the aubergines and courgettes in a roasting tray, season well, drizzle with 4 tbsp of olive oil and stir to coat.

3   Roast for 30 minutes, stirring once after 15 minutes, then add the sliced peppers and unpeeled garlic cloves. Cook for a further 15 minutes, stir again, and sprinkle in the cherry tomatoes, cut side up. Roast undisturbed for a further 30 minutes.

4   While the vegetables are roasting, place the sunflower seeds in a small roasting tin, stir in 1 tbsp of oil and sprinkle with salt. Place the tray on the bottom shelf of the oven and roast for 5 to 10 minutes, just until they start to swell and turn golden. Watch them carefully as they burn easily.

5   Carefully fold the chopped red onions and sunflower seeds into the roasted vegetables, transfer to a warm serving dish, and sprinkle with basil.

6   Serve immediately with the rouille.

Tip: The best way to deal with the roasted garlic cloves is to pick them up in your fingers and squeeze the buttery flesh on to bread, or scrape it out with your front teeth straight on to your tongue - not elegant, I admit, but oh so good! And needless to say, the rouille is just as garlicky and unsociable.

Chickpea and Sesame Purée with Stir-Fried Peppers

Serves 4

A hearty purée, reminiscent of the middle Eastern hummus, its potential heaviness lightened and brightened by a kick of fresh ginger and the toasted nuttiness of the sesame oil. It can be made in advance and refrigerated – in fact the flavours develop with keeping; add a couple of tablespoons of water and reheat it in a saucepan over very low heat or over a pan of boiling water. Check the seasoning again after reheating as the balance of flavours will change as it sits.

Tip: Toasted sesame oil has a much richer, nuttier flavour than raw sesame oil.

Ingredients

400g potatoes, peeled and cut into small pieces
2 tbsp and120ml toasted sesame oil
1 medium red and 1 medium yellow pepper, about 200g each, sliced into 1cm wide strips
250g onions, peeled and thickly sliced
30g ginger, peeled and cut into matchsticks
3 garlic cloves, peeled and crushed
2 x 400g tins chickpeas, drained and rinsed
2 tbsp light tahini (page 109)
15g fresh tarragon, coarsely chopped
Sea salt and freshly ground black pepper

Method

1 Boil the potatoes until tender, drain and mash.

2 Heat 2 tbsp of oil in a large frying pan, add the peppers, onions, ginger, garlic and some seasoning, and cook over low heat, stirring often, until the onions are golden and the peppers soft.

3 Blend the remaining sesame oil, chickpeas, tahini, 2 tbsp of water and some seasoning in a food processor until smooth. Add the mashed potatoes and pulse just enough to incorporate them. Check the seasoning.

4 Divide the purée between 4 warm plates and top with the peppers.

5 Sprinkle with tarragon and serve immediately.

Hazelnut Soup

Serves 2 as a main dish

Nuts may not sound like a natural basis for a soup but having eaten a chestnut soup in the Périgord region of France some years ago, I began experimenting and found that they produce a wonderfully voluptuous, deeply flavoured soup. In this recipe, the richness is offset by the smokiness of the pimentón and the acidity of the tomatoes.

Ingredients

3 tbsp toasted sesame oil
200g onions, peeled and coarsely chopped
2 garlic cloves, peeled and crushed
5g lemon thyme, coarsely chopped
1 tsp sweet smoked paprika (pimentón dulce) (see tip on page 128)
500ml water mixed with 1 tsp bouillon powder
200g chopped, toasted hazelnuts, finely ground in a food processor
Fresh lemon juice
Freshly grated nutmeg
1 x quantity Basic Cherry Tomato Salsa with parsley (page 23)
Plain soya yoghurt, well seasoned (page 52)
Sea salt and freshly ground black pepper

Method

1 Heat 2 tbsp of sesame oil in a medium saucepan, add the onions and garlic, and cook gently, stirring often, until they are soft and golden. Stir in the thyme and pimentón and cook for a further 5 minutes.

2 Add the stock mixture, hazelnuts and some seasoning, bring to the boil, turn the heat right down and simmer for 15 minutes. Cool slightly and blend until very smooth. Strain through a fine mesh sieve.

3 Return the soup to the saucepan, add a good squeeze of lemon juice and a generous scraping of nutmeg, and check the seasoning.

4 Stir the remaining sesame oil into the cherry tomato salsa and season.

5 Ladle the soup into warm bowls and add a good dollop of salsa and a swirl of yoghurt.

6 Serve immediately.

Tip: Make sure that you grind the hazelnuts really finely before adding them to the stock, or you will find that half of them get left in the sieve and the soup will have a coarse, grainy texture.

Cauliflower with a Difference

Serves 2

Cauliflower can be a challenging vegetable, with its decidedly delicate taste and its ability to change from perfectly al dente to mushy mess in a split second. It is however fairly versatile, its blandness and porous texture allowing it to soak up other stronger, more assertive flavours and acquire a bit of personality. Cheese is of course its traditional partner, but it is rare to come across cauliflower in any other shape or form except curried. This recipe has Mexican connotations, with its pickled jalapeño chillies and chipotle chilli, and it will change your image of cauliflower forever. The colour of the final dish is rather drab but a good handful of coriander sprinkled over the top makes up for its lack of looks.

Tip: Jars of Mexican vinegary, pickled jalapeño chillies are available in the world foods sections of supermarkets.

Ingredients

1 medium cauliflower, broken into florets
15 pitted green olives, halved
40g red onions, finely chopped
40g raisins, soaked in hot water for 30 minutes and squeezed dry
3 tbsp dark tahini (page 109)
1/2 lemon, juiced
30g flaked toasted almonds
15g pickled jalapeño chillies, seeded and chopped (see tip)
1/2 tsp chipotle chilli paste or powder (see tip on page 29)
2 tbsp olive oil
1 tbsp cumin seeds, toasted and coarsely ground (page 86)
10g fresh coriander, leaves only
Sea salt and freshly ground black pepper

Method

1   Steam the cauliflower until just tender – this will take about 10 minutes but it does depend on the age of the cauliflower and the size of the florets.

2   While the cauliflower is cooking, place all the remaining ingredients except the coriander in a roomy salad bowl and sprinkle in some seasoning. If the tahini is very dry and solid, add a bit of boiling water and mash it lightly with a fork – you are looking for a creamy consistency which will coat the cauliflower generously.

3   As soon as the cauliflower is ready, transfer it with a slotted spoon to the bowl and fold it in, taking care not to mash it.

4   Strew the coriander leaves over the top and serve immediately.

Fragrant Mushrooms

Serves 4

Button mushrooms are not one of my favourite ingredients as their flavour is fairly delicate and while sautéing them in plenty of olive oil and eating them on toast for breakfast is infinitely pleasurable, as the principal star in a main dish or as a vegetable, they need plenty of support from sparkier partners. This recipe allows their firm texture to shine while providing some Eastern promise from sesame, ginger and soy as well as a palate-tingling topping of chillies, cashews and mint. They are good with rice or Asian pastas like udon, soba and noodles.

Tip: Mushrooms tend to soak up moisture if they are washed, so unless they are very dirty, it is better to just rub them gently with a tea towel to remove any bits of soil which are clinging to them.

Ingredients

120ml toasted sesame oil
25g fresh ginger, peeled and sliced into matchsticks
375g onions, peeled and thickly sliced
4 large garlic cloves, peeled and crushed
450g button mushrooms, cleaned
2 tbsp rice wine vinegar
1/2 cup tamari or shoyu soy sauce (page 52)
1 tbsp agave nectar or honey (see tip on page 24)
1 tbsp wholegrain mustard
2 tbsp dark tahini (page 109)
1 large red chilli, deseeded and finely sliced
10g fresh mint, coarsely chopped
100g roasted cashew nuts, coarsely chopped
Freshly ground black pepper

Method

1   Heat the oil in a large heavy frying pan, add the ginger strips, onions and garlic, and stir-fry over medium heat for about five minutes, just until the onions start to wilt.

2   Stir in the mushrooms and cook for a further five minutes.

3   Add the vinegar, soy sauce, agave and mustard, turn up the heat and cook fairly briskly, stirring regularly, until the mushrooms have absorbed most of the moisture. Stir in the tahini and some black pepper. Check the seasoning. It is unlikely that you will need any salt as the soy sauce is salty.

4   In a small bowl, mix together the chilli, mint and cashews and sprinkle over the mushrooms.

5   Serve immediately.

Fried Plantains with Pumpkin Seed Sauce

Serves 2

Although plantains originated in Asia, they are a very popular and traditional ingredient in Mexican cuisine, contributed by the African slaves who were shipped to the port of Veracruz on the Gulf of Mexico. Unlike bananas, they are not eaten raw and need to be allowed to ripen until the skins are deep yellow and patched with black, and the flesh is soft to the touch – so buy them well ahead of time and leave them somewhere warm to mature for a week or even two. Their flavour is starchier and less sweet than bananas, but frying them in a bit of oil gives them a delicious hint of caramel.

Tip: Pumpkin seeds, which have been used to thicken Mexican sauces since pre-Hispanic times, are full of essential fatty acids and minerals, and are a good source of protein. They are also reputed to lower cholesterol and reduce inflammation.

Ingredients

90g pumpkin seeds
1 x quantity Roasted Tomato Sauce (page 24)
1 tsp chipotle chilli paste or powder (see tip on page 29)
3 large ripe plantains, about 250g each
3 tbsp olive oil
10g fresh flat leaf parsley, coarsely chopped
Tortilla chips or cooked rice, to serve (optional)
Sea salt and freshly ground black pepper

Method

1   Place the pumpkin seeds in a heavy frying pan over medium heat and cook, stirring constantly, until they pop and just start to brown – 4 to 5 minutes. Be careful not to let them scorch or the sauce will be bitter.

2   Cool slightly and set 2 tbsp aside for the garnish. Grind the remainder finely in a food processor.

3   Heat the tomato sauce, add the chipotle chilli paste and some seasoning, and cook over medium heat for 5 minutes.

4   Peel the plantains, halve them lengthways and then cut them across so that you have four roughly equal lengths.

5   Heat the oil in a non-stick frying pan, add the plantain slices and cook them over medium heat for about 3 minutes on each side, until they are lightly golden. Drain on kitchen paper.

6 Stir the ground pumpkin seeds into the sauce and spread it in a warm, shallow serving dish. Top with the plantains and sprinkle with the reserved pumpkin seeds and parsley.

7 Serve immediately with tortilla chips or rice.

Pasta with Spiced Cashew Sauce

Serves 2

The flavours in this sauce are decidedly Eastern, and a pasta such as the Japanese udon or soba, or Chinese noodles, would be more appropriate than pasta shells or penne. However, after numerous experiments, I have taken the Italian route, simply because hollow pasta shapes, like the shells and penne, trap the sauce and distribute it throughout the dish. With smooth strands of pasta, on the other hand, the sauce glides off and although it is still all very delicious, you end up with most of the sauce in the bottom of the bowl and no pasta with which to eat it!

Ingredients

200g roasted cashews
2 tbsp tamari or shoyu soy sauce (page 52)
4 tbsp toasted sesame or walnut oil
300g wholemeal pasta shells or penne
1 tbsp each cumin and coriander seeds, toasted and finely ground (page 86)
1 tsp ground cinnamon
1 red and 1 green chilli, deseeded and finely chopped
2 garlic cloves, peeled and crushed
3 tbsp fresh lemon juice
6 fat spring onions, finely sliced
10g chives, coarsely snipped with scissors
Freshly ground black pepper

Method

1 Place the cashews, soy sauce, oil and some black pepper in a food processor and process until fairly smooth – you don't want a purée but neither do you want large chunks of nuts.

2 Cook the pasta in plenty of boiling salted water according to the manufacturer's instructions. Reserve 125ml of the water, then drain well and return to the saucepan. Add the reserved water, cashew mixture, spices, chillies, garlic, lemon juice, spring onions and chives and toss to mix well. Check the seasoning – it is unlikely to need any salt as the nuts and soy sauce are salty.

3 Divide between two warm bowls and serve immediately.

Tip: The overall heat of the dish depends on the chillies. If you are a fire-eater, a couple of bird's eyes or Scotch bonnets will light the whole dish to the required degree of conflagration; and if you prefer something more subtle, then the mildest of chillies will provide sufficient warmth and spice - but don't be tempted to leave the chillies out altogether, as the sauce will be flat-tasting.

need2know

Torta of Refried Beans, Avocado and Chipotle Mayonnaise

Makes 4 tortas

A torta is a Mexican sandwich, traditionally made in a large flattish roll known as a telera, and certainly a big bread roll is essential, as a torta is a meal in itself, well filled and deeply savoury and satisfying.

Ingredients

5 tbsp olive oil
125g onions, peeled and coarsely chopped
2 garlic cloves, peeled and crushed
1 tbsp cumin seeds, toasted and finely ground (page 86)
1 x 400g tin black or red kidney beans, rinsed and well drained
2 small ripe avocadoes
40g red onions, peeled and coarsely chopped
Fresh lime juice
5g fresh coriander, coarsely chopped
4 ciabatta or similar bread rolls
1 x quantity nut cheese made with pine nuts (page 87)
1 tsp chipotle chilli powder or paste (see tip on page 29)
2 large tomatoes, about 100g each, cut into 4 slices each
Sea salt and freshly ground black pepper

Tip: Tortas do not make for elegant eating, so be sure to provide plenty of paper napkins!

Method

1   Heat 1 tbsp of olive oil in a frying pan, add the onions, one garlic clove and some salt and pepper and cook, stirring occasionally, until they just start to brown. Stir in the cumin and cook for 1 minute longer. Add the beans and mash them coarsely with a potato masher or a large fork. Check the seasoning.

2   Coarsely mash the avocadoes with the second garlic clove, red onions, remaining olive oil, 1 tbsp lime juice and some salt and pepper in a bowl. Stir in the coriander, check the seasoning and add more lime juice if the flavour needs brightening.

3   Split the rolls. Stir the chilli powder into the nut cheese and spread over the cut sides of the bread. Divide the refried beans between the four bottoms, then spoon the avocado mixture on top. Finish off with two slices of tomato and a good sprinkling of salt and pepper. Place the bread lid on top and press down gently.

4   Serve within 30 minutes.

Walnut and Olive Pâté with Fresh Fig Chutney

Serves 8

An interesting combination of flavours here, with the savoury, almost intensely nutty and briny terrine contrasting with the sparkling, lively chutney. It makes a lovely summer lunch, with a salad, or an unusual first course, with the added bonus that both the terrine and chutney can be made ahead of time.

Ingredients

Tip: While the fig chutney is a perfect accompaniment to the terrine, the plum chutney on page 110 works equally well when purple figs are not in season.

400ml red wine vinegar
200g light muscovado sugar
150g red onions, peeled and coarsely chopped
2 garlic cloves, peeled and crushed
25g fresh ginger, peeled and finely grated
1 orange, zest and juice
1 cinnamon stick
2 star anise
1/4 tsp chilli flakes
450g ripe purple figs, destalked and diced
2 tbsp pomegranate molasses (see tip on page 73)
500g firm tofu, drained (page 52)
1 garlic clove, peeled
1/4 cup light tahini (page 109)
2 tsp tamari or shoyu soy sauce (page 52)
5g sage leaves
25g flat leaf parsley
1 tbsp fresh lemon juice, or to taste
150g walnuts, toasted and coarsely chopped (page 86)
30 black olives, pitted and coarsely chopped
1 tbsp finely chopped flat leaf parsley
Sea salt and freshly ground black pepper
500ml bowl or loaf tin

Method

1   For the chutney, combine the first nine ingredients in a saucepan and bring to the boil, stirring to dissolve the sugar. Turn the heat right down and leave to simmer for about 40 minutes, stirring occasionally, until it becomes thick and syrupy. Add the figs and continue to cook until they are soft but still holding their shape, about 20 minutes. Stir in the molasses and leave to cool. The chutney will keep in the refrigerator for 10 days.

2   In a food processor, blend the tofu, garlic clove, tahini, soy sauce, herbs, 1 tbsp of lemon juice and some seasoning until smooth. Scrape into a bowl and fold in the nuts and olives. Check the seasoning, adding more lemon juice if the flavour is a bit flat.

3   Brush a 500ml bowl with oil and line it with cling film, smoothing it out as much as possible. Pack the nut mixture into the bowl and level the top. Refrigerate until firm, at least 1 hour and up to 3 days. Turn out onto a serving dish and sprinkle with chopped parsley.

4   Serve the pâté with the chutney.

Tip: Tahini is a paste of sesame seeds and is used extensively in Middle Eastern cuisine. It comes in three varieties: 'white', made with raw sesame seeds, fairly bland and not readily available; 'light', where the sesame seeds are hulled before toasting, resulting in a delicate flavour; and 'dark', rich and strong due to the unhulled toasted sesame seeds. Light and dark tahini are available in supermarkets.

Nut Roast with Plum and Cranberry Chutney

Serves 4

Nut roast may be horribly 1970s, but it is a classic and oh so delicious, particularly when served with a flamboyant sweet and sour chutney. The list of ingredients is long and the preparation does take time, but both the roast and chutney can be prepared in advance so all that is needed is a bit of forward thinking and organisation.

Ingredients

Tip: This nut roast does not slice particularly well so it is a good idea to present it whole on a large platter and massacre it at the table.

2 tbsp olive oil
200g onions, peeled and finely chopped
75g red pepper, diced
75g yellow pepper, diced
75g carrots, peeled and diced
4 garlic cloves, peeled and crushed
100g walnuts, toasted (page 86)
125g soft wholemeal bread
5g fresh thyme leaves
5g parsley
200g mixed nuts, toasted
2 tbsp bouillon powder
150ml water
60g red onions, peeled and coarsely chopped
20g fresh ginger, peeled and coarsely grated
1 tbsp black mustard seeds
5 whole cloves
1 cinnamon stick
325g purple plums, stoned and chopped
1/4 tsp chilli flakes
50g dried cranberries
100g granulated sugar
3 tbsp cider vinegar
Sea salt and freshly ground black pepper
1 x 500g loaf tin, brushed with oil and the bottom lined with baking parchment

Method

1   Heat 1 tbsp of oil in a large frying pan, add the onions, peppers, carrots and 2 crushed garlic cloves, and cook over medium heat, stirring regularly, until soft and lightly coloured. Grind the toasted walnuts finely in a food processor. Add the bread and herbs and process again until the herbs are finely chopped. Add the mixed nuts and pulse two or three times to chop them medium coarse. Stir into the vegetables in the frying pan and grind in some black pepper. Pour in the water, sprinkle with bouillon powder and mix it all together gently with a spatula. Check the seasoning and add a bit of salt if needed – the bouillon is salty so it may be enough. Pack into the loaf tin and smooth the top.

2   The nut roast can be prepared up to this point several hours ahead.

3   For the chutney, heat the remaining tbsp of oil in a medium saucepan, add the red onions, ginger and remaining garlic, and cook gently, stirring often, until wilted and soft. Mix in the mustard seeds, cloves and cinnamon, and cook for a further five minutes.

4   Add the plums, chilli flakes, cranberries, sugar and vinegar, turn the heat right down and leave to simmer until the plums have broken down and you have a lovely magenta coloured chutney. Cool before serving. The chutney will keep for up to 5 days in the refrigerator.

5   Preheat the oven to 180°C/350°F/Gas Mark 4/fan oven 160°C and bake the nut roast for 40 minutes. Cool for 10 minutes before turning out onto a serving dish.

6   Serve hot or cold with the chutney.

Gianduia Ice Cream

Gianduia is a heavenly concoction of chocolate and toasted hazelnuts, which was developed by Italian chocolatiers, Caffarel, in the early 19th century and has become a speciality of the city of Turin. It is intensely flavoured and hopelessly moreish, so beware of this ice cream and serve it in small quantities as it is utterly wicked!

Ingredients

400ml tinned coconut milk (see tip)
100g dark chocolate (70% minimum cocoa solids), chopped
75g hazelnut butter
50g caster sugar
1 tsp vanilla extract
Fresh berries, to serve (optional)

Tip: Coconut milk is available in tins in most supermarkets. Although it is rich with a good creamy texture, it has little flavour and is therefore very flexible.

Method

1 Heat the milk in a medium saucepan until steaming. Add the chocolate and stir until melted. Whisk in the hazelnut butter, sugar and vanilla. Set aside to cool.

2 Churn in an ice cream machine according to the manufacturer's instructions and freeze until needed. Soften in the refrigerator for 15 minutes before scooping.

3 Serve the ice cream with berries.

6

Fresh Herbs – Aroma and Fragrance

A leisurely stroll around a herb garden, let alone a whole farm, is a feast for the senses as well as a revelation. While supermarkets nowadays offer fresh herbs in packets, bunches and pots, the selection is but a glimmer of the infinite variety of flavours, aromas and textures which the herb world has to offer. Their fragrant magic can transform an utterly ordinary dish into something very special and make it taste of Tuscany and Provence, of Mexico and India, of an English country garden or a sun-baked mountainside. A proper foray into the perfumed world of herbs will take you on a global tour, both culinary and medicinal, a journey of discovery through myriads of variations of every family – Moroccan mint, Korean mint, Corsican mint, Tashkent mint, chocolate mint, apple mint, spearmint, catmint, peppermint, emperor's mint, Cunningham mint, Logee's mint – the list seems endless, and although they will all taste of mint, each and every flavour will be different and will bring its own appeal and enchantment to your cooking as you toss a herb by the handful into salads, blend it into vivid vibrant sauces, roast it with vegetables or swirl it into soups; in one recipe, you can make herbs the star of the show, in another a subtle background note – they are truly multitalented, as well as forgiving: I have found it difficult to make mistakes in my use of herbs, as some combinations and partnerships may prove to be more successful than others, but only very rarely has an experiment proved unpleasant, and never inedible.

The term 'herb' is used to describe the 'live' part of the plant, i.e. its stem, leaves and very occasionally roots (coriander), and should not be confused with the seeds, dried fruit, bark or kernel, for instance, as in fennel seeds, allspice berries, cinnamon and peppercorns, which are classed as spices.

While the most common herbs are readily available, it is great fun growing your own as they do not take up much room and their prowess in the kitchen is enhanced by utter freshness. Furthermore, harvesting your own herbs from a pot on a sunny windowsill or a patch in the garden will not only increase the flavour but also your pleasure in the food you prepare. In addition, being exposed to sun, rain, frost and other weather vagaries boosts the natural oil content in the plants, thereby making them even more aromatic. I have found from experience that growing herbs from seed can be a challenge and prefer to buy them in pots, making them easier to nurture.

Tip:
Although pesto keeps well, the longer it sits, the dimmer its colour and the stronger its flavour.

Pesto

This vegan pesto has countless uses and can be varied with different herbs and nuts.

Ingredients

120ml olive oil
15g basil
1 garlic clove, peeled
150g raw pine nuts
1 tsp Dijon mustard
1 tsp bouillon powder
Sea salt and freshly ground black pepper

Method

Purée all the ingredients together in a food processor until fairly smooth. If the mixture is very thick, add about 1 tbsp of water to loosen it.

Pineapple and Avocado Salad

Serves 4

This is a fresh and energising salad, with wonderful contrasts of texture and flavour, rich and creamy, sharp and crunchy, hot and sweet. I have to admit the avocado fan is decidedly 'nouvelle cuisine', but it does look pretty! If, however, you cannot bear to be associated with this kind of presentation, simply peel and stone the avocado, dice it and mix it with the other ingredients.

Ingredients

20g hulled pumpkin seeds
1 tsp and 2 tbsp olive oil
225g peeled, diced fresh pineapple
25g red onions, peeled and finely sliced
1 lime, juiced
1 red or green chilli, deseeded and finely sliced
2 small ripe avocadoes
10g basil, shredded
1/2 tsp chipotle chilli powder (page 29)
Sea salt and freshly ground black pepper

Method

1   Heat the oven to 180°C/350°F/Gas Mark 4/fan oven 160°C. Place the pumpkin seeds in a small baking dish and stir in 1 tsp of olive oil and 1/4 tsp of salt. Roast for about 7 minutes, until the seeds are slightly swollen and barely starting to brown. Cool.

2   In a small bowl, mix the remaining olive oil, pineapple, onions, lime juice and chillies, and season with salt and pepper.

3   Halve and stone the avocadoes, and peel off the skin with a sharp knife. Lay the halves on a chopping board hollow side down and slice through them 4 or 5 times at an angle, leaving them attached at the narrow end. With the palm of your hand, flatten each half gently so that the slices fan out.

4   Slide a spatula under the fans and place them on four plates.

5   Spoon the pineapple mixture over them, and sprinkle with basil and the roasted pumpkin seeds. Dust lightly with chilli powder.

6   Serve immediately before the avocado loses its colour.

Tip: It is always best to buy hard avocadoes and ripen them at home, as those which are soft and yielding before purchase are likely to have dark patches on the inside. An avocado takes about 3 days to ripen at room temperature and can then be stored in the vegetable drawer of the refrigerator until needed.

Spiced Pumpkin Soup with Pumpkin Seed Salsa

Serves 4

Pumpkins are thin on flavour and texture, and I must admit to a weekly wisp of despair during the autumn when I unpack my organic box and find yet another pumpkin or squash lurking in the bottom, defying me to cudgel my brain and imagination in order to develop a new recipe. But there is a solution: cook it with oil until it is golden and caramelised, and its wishy washy flavour will concentrate to a honeyed sweetness. This same sweetness cries out for sharp, acidic partners like limes, yoghurt and tomatoes and the bold assertive heat of a fiery chilli.

Ingredients

Tip: Coconut cream comes in tins and in solid blocks. The blocks have a considerably stronger flavour.

1.5 kg pumpkin, peeled, seeded and cut into 2 cm chunks
3 tbsp and 1 tsp olive oil
150g onions, peeled and coarsely chopped
1 tsp bouillon powder or 1/2 vegetable stock cube, crumbled
100g solid coconut cream, coarsley chopped (see tip)
1 x 400g tin black beans, rinsed and drained
Fresh lemon juice
20g pumpkin seeds
1 x quantity Basic Cherry Tomato Salsa with chives (page 23)
Plain soya yoghurt, well seasoned, to serve (page 52)
Sea salt and freshly ground black pepper

Method

1   Preheat the oven to 200°C/400°F/Gas Mark 6/fan oven 180°C.

2   Place the pumpkin in a roasting tin, drizzle with 2 tbsp of olive oil, season well and roast in the oven, stirring every 10 minutes or so, until it is soft and golden around the edges, about 45 minutes.

3   While the pumpkin is cooking, heat 1 tbsp of olive oil in a medium saucepan and add the onions. Cook, stirring occasionally, until they start to brown, about 20 minutes.

4   When the pumpkin is ready, transfer it to the onion saucepan and pour in enough water to cover it. Bring to the boil and simmer for 10 minutes.

5 Cool slightly before puréeing in a food processor or blender until smooth and velvety. Return the soup to the saucepan and add the bouillon powder or stock cube, enough water to make it the consistency of double cream, and half the coconut cream. Bring to the boil, stirring to melt the coconut. Taste the soup and add more coconut if necessary – you are looking for a faint whiff of coconut, rather than a distinct flavour, and the proportions depend on the sweetness of the pumpkin. Stir in the beans and check the seasoning. Squeeze in some lemon juice if the flavour is at all cloying, but only enough to cut the sweetness as the salsa and yoghurt will add more acidity and one of this soup's many charms is the sweet and sharp contrast.

6 Heat 1 tsp of olive oil in a small heavy frying pan. Add the pumpkin seeds and some salt, and cook over medium heat, stirring often, until the seeds start to pop and smell nutty. Remove from the heat and cool.

7 When the soup is ready, mix the pumpkin seeds with the salsa.

8 Ladle the soup into four warm bowls, add a good spoonful of salsa and drizzle it all with some yoghurt.

9 Serve immediately, adding more salsa and yoghurt to the soup as you eat it.

Spring Vegetable Laksa

Serves 2 as a main dish

Recipes and variations of laksa abound throughout South East Asia but it is perhaps most at home in Singapore and Malaysia. In its simplest form, it is nothing more than noodles in a coconut sauce or 'gravy'; at the other end of the spectrum, it can reach the height of culinary sophistication. In all cases, it is fragrant and aromatic, rich with coconut and curry spices, and full of deep, bright flavours. It normally contains noodles, or sometimes rice, making it a one-pot meal. And so long as you have a food processor or electric mini-chopper for the basic paste, it takes only minutes to make. I love to add plenty of tamarind pulp to my laksa, to give it a bright, citrusy jolt which cuts through the heat of the spices and the richness and sweetness of the coconut. Start off by adding just a heaped teaspoon and taste the laksa before adding any more.

Tip: Lemongrass is quite tough and needs to be chopped very finely as a coarse texture results in a mouthful of horrible, sharp bits!

Ingredients

100g brown basmati rice

3 garlic cloves, peeled

2 stalks lemongrass, outer layers removed and heart very finely chopped

175g onions, peeled and coarsely chopped

25g fresh ginger, peeled and coarsely chopped

2 hottish red chillies, halved and deseeded

4 tbsp toasted sesame oil

1 tbsp cumin seeds, toasted and coarsely ground (page 86)

1 cinnamon stick

1 tbsp tamari or shoyu soy sauce (page 52)

2 x 400g tins coconut milk

2 oranges, grated rind and juice

2 limes, grated rind and juice

1 tsp of tamarind paste or to taste (see tip on page 150)

1 tsp bouillon powder

50g solid coconut cream, coarsely chopped

150g frozen broad beans, skinned

150g frozen peas

125g slender asparagus tips, cooked

15g fresh tarragon, coarsely chopped

15g mint, coarsely chopped

Sea salt and freshly ground black pepper

Method

1 Cook the rice in plenty of boiling salted water for 50 minutes. Drain well and set aside.

2 While the rice is cooking, make the laksa paste by placing the garlic, lemongrass, onions, ginger and chillies in an electric mini chopper or food processor and pulse until everything is very finely chopped.

3 Heat the sesame oil in a medium saucepan, add the laksa paste and ground cumin, and cook gently, stirring often, until the mixture starts to brown.

4 Stir in the cinnamon stick, soy sauce, coconut milk, orange juice and the juice of one lime, taramind, bouillon powder and some seasoning, and bring to the boil.

5 Turn the heat right down and leave to simmer for 20 minutes.

6 Add the coconut cream and simmer for a further two or three minutes, until it has melted.

7 Stir in the lime and orange rinds and rice, and reheat until steaming. If it is rather thick, add some more water or stock to achieve a soupy rather than porridgey consistency.

8 Add the vegetables, and check the seasoning and the sweet/acid balance, adding more lime juice and/or tamarind if it tastes a bit flat – it all depends on how juicy and sweet the oranges were.

9 Stir in the chopped herbs and serve immediately in deep warm bowls.

Minted Pea Hummus

Serves 4

Whilst the word 'hummus' means chickpeas in Arabic and therefore my bright green, aromatic purée cannot really be called a hummus, it is, after all, made with peas of some sort and the texture is similar, faintly starchy and grainy, although lighter and fresher, lacking the robustness of the traditional chickpea and tahini mixture.

It is difficult to give exact quantities and weights for peas in their pods as some pods will invariably be full to bursting and others contain nothing more than two or three peas the size of a peppercorn, so it is better to buy plenty. You will need about a kilo of podded peas, and while fresh peas are one of summer's joys, they do require a certain amount of effort, so if you are short of time, frozen petits pois work extremely well.

Tip: Do not be tempted to make the hummus too far in advance, as the lemon juice will turn the bright green colour to khaki over time - two or three hours is really the maximum.

Ingredients

1 kg fresh peas, podded or 500g frozen petits pois
100ml and 2 tbsp olive oil
2 large garlic cloves, peeled
20g fresh mint, leaves only
2 lemons, juiced
50g red onions, peeled and finely chopped
1 large mild red chilli, seeded and thinly sliced
15 pitted black olives, halved
1/2 tsp sweet paprika
1 1/2 tsp cumin seeds, toasted and coarsely ground (page 86)
Lemon wedges (optional)
Pitta bread or French bread to serve
Sea salt and freshly ground black pepper

Method

1. Cook the fresh peas in plenty of salted, boiling water until tender; the time will depend on the age of the peas but test after 5 minutes. If you are using frozen peas, cook them for 3 minutes.

2. Drain and refresh under cold running water. Drain again and turn out onto a clean, dry dishcloth to get rid of any excess water.

3. Transfer to a food processor, add the 100ml of olive oil, garlic, three quarters of the mint, 2 tbsp of lemon juice and some seasoning, and process until smooth.

4. Taste and sharpen with additional lemon juice if the flavour is not bright enough.

5. Scrape the hummus into a wide, shallow bowl.

6. Chop the remaining mint coarsely.

7. Drizzle the hummus with the 2 tbsp of olive oil, sprinkle with red onions, chilli, olives and mint, and finally dust with paprika and cumin.

8. Garnish with lemon wedges and serve.

Gazpacho Jelly

Serves 4

Gazpacho – fresh, cool, aromatic, sharp with vinegar and hot with raw onions and garlic – is an intrinsic part of a holiday in Spain generally, and most particularly Andalucía. Modern 'convenience' foods like tinned tomatoes have somewhat ruined its reputation, and of course the name is often used now to describe any kind of cold soup containing raw chopped vegetables. In the recipe below, I have recreated a dish I first came across countless years ago at La Petite Cuisine School of Cooking in Richmond. It was called 'Gazpacho en gelée' – a French name always sounded so much more sophisticated! – and was served with a garlic mayonnaise.

Ingredients

275g ripe tomatoes
1 tbsp sun-dried tomato purée
1 tsp sherry vinegar
3 garlic cloves, peeled
1/2 tsp bouillon powder
1 sachet Vege-Gel (see tip)
2 tbsp olive oil
40g each red and yellow pepper, diced
70g cucumber, seeded and diced
30g red onions, finely chopped
5g flat leaf parsley, finely chopped
Sea salt and freshly ground black pepper
1 x quantity aïoli (page 87)
Black olives, to serve
Thin slices of French bread, brushed with oil and grilled until crisp, to serve
4 x 60ml metal ramekins, lightly oiled

Tip: Gelatine is made from cows' hooves and is therefore never used in vegan cuisine. Having experimented with various seaweed-based gelling agents, I have found that Vege-Gel, widely available in supermarkets, is the easiest one to use. It sets quite solidly so it is a good idea to bring any jelly made with it back to room temperature before serving.

Method

1   Blend the tomatoes, purée, vinegar, garlic, bouillon powder and some seasoning until smooth. Strain through a medium mesh sieve into a small saucepan. Sprinkle with Vege-Gel and set aside for 10 minutes. Stir the mixture to ensure the Vege-Gel has completely dissolved.

2   Heat, stirring constantly, until just below boiling point. Remove from the heat and add the olive oil, the diced vegetables and parsley and mix well. Spoon into the ramekins and refrigerate until set, at least 2 hours or overnight. Bring back to room temperature before serving.

3   To un-mould the jellies, dip the ramekins very briefly into hot water and turn the jellies out onto four plates.

4   Serve with the aïoli, olives and bread.

Sweet and Sour Artichokes

Serves 2

Artichokes can be time-consuming and fiddly to prepare, and my favourite way to serve them is simply to boil them until the outer leaves pull out easily and then eat them with nothing more than some excellent extra virgin olive oil. But they are also very seasonal and their arrival at my local greengrocer heralds warm weather and long sunny days, which encourages me to indulge in them at every opportunity during their short visit. For this dish, you need quite a lot of artichokes, which have to be cooked and the leaves and choke removed, so don't try to prepare them when you are running late and feeling tired and intolerant!

Tip: Citrus zesters are available in kitchen shops and are an excellent investment, as they produce long thin strands of zest full of essential oils and citrusy aroma. The Good Grips one works well.

Ingredients

6 large globe artichokes, stems removed
150g cherry tomatoes, halved
1 tsp and 6 tbsp olive oil
150g onions, peeled and coarsely chopped
2 garlic cloves, peeled and crushed
25g sultanas or raisins
120ml white wine
5 tbsp sweet Marsala wine
1/4 tsp crushed chilli flakes
1 small orange, zest and juice
Needles from 2 bushy rosemary sprigs, finely chopped
2 tbsp thyme leaves, finely chopped
1/2 tsp saffron threads
10g chives, finely snipped with scissors
2 thick slices of heavy bread, toasted
25g shelled pistachios, toasted and coarsely chopped (page 86)
Sea salt and freshly ground black pepper

Method

1 Steam the artichokes for about 30 minutes, until the outer leaves pull away easily. Cool slightly and carefully remove the leaves – rubber gloves are a great asset here, as the inner artichoke will keep its heat for a long time. With a small teaspoon, scrape away the choke.

2 Slice the artichoke bottoms about 3mm thick and set aside.

3 While the artichokes are cooking, preheat the oven to 200°C/400°F/Gas Mark 6/ fan oven 180°C.

4 Arrange the cherry tomatoes cut side up on a baking tray lined with foil, drizzle with 1 tsp of olive oil, season well and cook on the top shelf of the oven until they are slightly shrivelled and just starting to blacken along the edges, 20 to 30 minutes.

5 Heat 3 tbsp of olive oil in a heavy frying pan, add the onions and garlic, and cook over medium heat, stirring occasionally, until they start to brown, about 15 minutes.

6 Add the sultanas, white wine, Marsala, chilli, orange juice and some seasoning, and boil briskly until most of the liquid has evaporated.

7 Stir in the herbs, saffron, sliced artichokes and tomatoes, and bring back to simmering point.

8 Toss in the orange zest, remaining olive oil and chives, and check the seasoning.

9 Place the toasted bread on two warm plates and spoon the artichokes over it.

10 Sprinkle with pistachios and serve immediately.

Baked Mushrooms Florentine

Serves 2

'Florentine' has become synonymous with spinach and a cheese sauce of one sort or another, the best known combination perhaps being Eggs Florentine, where the eggs are baked on a bed of spinach and topped with the cheese sauce – very 1970s! In this recipe, the mushrooms serve as a bed for the spinach, which is spiked with sun-dried tomatoes and enriched with basil and pine nuts.

Ingredients

Tip: The skin on portabello mushrooms is quite thick and tends to toughen with cooking so it is always best to peel them.

300g fresh spinach, washed and drained
2 tbsp olive oil
175g onions, peeled and coarsely chopped
1 x quantity pesto (page 114)
5 sun-dried tomatoes in olive oil, drained and diced
4 large portabello mushrooms, about 50g each, peeled
100g wholemeal breadcrumbs mixed with 1 tbsp olive oil
Sea salt and freshly ground black pepper

Method

1 Cook the spinach over high heat in a large frying pan until wilted and dark green. Transfer to a strainer and press out as much moisture as possible with the back of a wooden spoon before chopping coarsely.

2 Rinse out the frying pan and heat the olive oil in it. Add the onions and cook, stirring occasionally, until soft and translucent, about 15 minutes.

3 Stir the spinach, pesto and sun-dried tomatoes into the onions and check the seasoning. Divide the mixture between the mushrooms, smoothing and spreading it to the edge with a teaspoon. Pat the breadcrumbs on top of the spinach.

4 Place the mushrooms in a roasting tin and bake in a preheated oven at 200°C/400°F/ Gas Mark 6/fan oven 180°C until the breadcrumbs are golden, about 15 minutes.

5 Serve immediately.

Wild Mushroom Spaghetti

Serves 2

A dish sublime in its utter simplicity, which I learned from a client who is brave enough to pick her own chanterelles. Although the wild mushrooms require a certain financial investment, they are worth every mouthful. You can use just one type of mushroom, like chanterelles or girolles, or a packet of the mixed wild mushrooms available at many large supermarkets.

Ingredients

6 tbsp olive oil
2 garlic cloves, chopped
250g wild mushrooms, thoroughly cleaned and coarsely chopped (see tip)
250g wholemeal spaghetti
10g flat leaf parsley, coarsely chopped
Sea salt and freshly ground black pepper

Method

1 Heat 4 tbsp of olive oil in a large frying pan and add the garlic. Stir over medium heat until it starts to brown. Add the mushrooms and plenty of seasoning, turn the heat up and fry briskly, stirring often, until any moisture has evaporated and the mushrooms are sizzling.

2 Cook the spaghetti according to the instructions on the packet and drain thoroughly. Add to the frying pan along with the remaining olive oil and parsley and toss well.

3 Check the seasoning and serve immediately.

Tip: Wild mushrooms tend to be full of grit and even bits of fern and leaves. The ideal way to clean them is to use a soft brush - there are specialist mushroom brushes but a toothbrush works just as well and is much cheaper. However, sometimes they are so dirty that only washing under cold running water will do, but be quick about it as they absorb moisture easily and once they are waterlogged, require much longer cooking.

Aubergine and Roasted Pepper Caviar

Serves 2

Recipes for aubergine purées abound throughout the Middle East and Mediterranean. It is widely known as 'poor man's caviar', and like many traditional dishes, there is no one hard and fast list of ingredients or method for preparing it. The ideal way to cook the aubergines is to grill them on a charcoal BBQ, as this imparts a subtle, delicious smokiness to the purée. A good alternative is to impale the aubergines on a large kitchen fork and hold them over a gas flame, but the easiest method of all is simply to bake them in the oven.

Tip: Smoked paprika, pimentón, comes in two varieties, sweet (dulce), and hot (picante), which will give the caviar a kick of heat. The choice is yours.

Ingredients

450g aubergines
1 garlic clove, peeled
10g parsley, coarsely chopped
1/2 tsp sweet or hot smoked paprika (pimentón dulce or picante) (see tip)
2 tbsp cumin seeds, toasted and medium ground (page 86)
40g dark tahini (page 109)
6 tbsp olive oil
Fresh lemon juice
1 small red and 1 small yellow pepper, about 175g each, grilled
20g pine nuts, toasted (page 86)
125ml plain soya yoghurt, well seasoned (page 52)
1 garlic clove, peeled and crushed
10g fresh mint, coarsely chopped
Pitta bread, to serve
Sea salt and freshly ground black pepper

Method

1   Preheat the oven to 200°C/400°F/Gas Mark 6/fan oven 180°C.

2   Place the aubergines on a baking tray and bake until totally soft, about 1 hour. Cool slightly and peel – the skin will come off easily in strips.

3   Squeeze the aubergine flesh gently to extract as much liquid as possible, then purée in a food processor with the whole garlic, parsley, pimentón, cumin, tahini, 4 tbsp of olive oil, some seasoning and about 1 tbsp of fresh lemon juice. Add a bit more lemon juice if the flavour is not quite bright enough.

4 Skin the peppers and cut the flesh into 1cm pieces. Fold into the aubergine mixture and scrape it all into a wide, shallow serving dish. Sprinkle with pine nuts.

5 Mix the yoghurt, crushed garlic, mint and remaining olive oil in a small bowl and season. Drizzle over the caviar.

6 Serve immediately with warm pitta bread and extra yoghurt on the side.

Savoury Chickpeas with Oregano Pesto

Serves 4

Tip: This recipe works equally well with other pulses like butter beans and flageolets, but avoid the stronger tasting red kidney and black beans. And feel free to substitute sunflower seeds or pine nuts for the pumpkin seeds.

Although the tomatoes take time to cook and acquire the wonderful caramelised sweetness which roasting imparts, this is a quick and easy dish to prepare, a satisfying supper after a long hard day when you don't really want to go to a lot of trouble: once the tomatoes are in the oven, it is just a matter of chopping and cooking the onions, and slinging all the ingredients for the pesto into a food processor. You will probably even have time to spare while you wait for the tomatoes to reach the desired softness and colour – ten minutes to do a few energising yoga stretches, listen to your phone messages, go through your personal post, or pour yourself a welcome glass of wine!

Ingredients

400g tomatoes, quartered
4 tbsp olive oil
300g red onions, peeled and sliced
25g fresh oregano
50g rocket
2 garlic cloves, peeled
150g firm tofu (page 52)
120ml olive oil
2 tbsp white wine
1 tbsp wholegrain mustard
50g pumpkin seeds
1 tbsp of pumpkin butter (optional)
2 x 400g tins chickpeas, rinsed
125g frozen petits pois, defrosted
Salt and freshly ground black pepper

Method

1　Place the tomatoes in a baking dish, drizzle with 1 tbsp of olive oil, season well, and cook in a preheated oven at 220°C/450°F/Gas Mark 7/fan oven 200°C for 30 to 40 minutes, until they are soft and brown around the edges.

2　While the tomatoes are cooking, heat the remaining 3 tbsp of olive oil in a large frying pan, add the onions, and cook over low heat, stirring occasionally, until lightly browned, about 20 minutes.

3　For the pesto, strip the oregano leaves from the stalks and place them in the bowl of a food processor with the rocket, garlic, tofu, 120ml of olive oil, wine, mustard and some seasoning and process until fairly smooth. Add the pumpkin seeds and butter and process again very briefly to break them down a bit. Check the seasoning and set aside.

4　Add the chickpeas and petit pois to the onions, along with some seasoning, and stir-fry for a few minutes to heat them up. Carefully fold in the roasted tomatoes.

5　Top with some pesto and serve immediately.

Butter bean Purée with Spiced Aubergines and Sun-Dried Tomato Salsa

Serves 4

The aubergine's spongy, pallid flesh is such a disappointment compared to its smooth, glossy outerwear! It is an exotic-looking vegetable, its deep purple skin promising wealth and wonder which does not materialise unless it is carefully and considerately cooked. But give it plenty of oil – extra virgin olive, toasted sesame, walnut or hazelnut – and a modest squirt of acidity – vinegar, whether rice, wine, cider or balsamic, and fresh lemon and lime – and the dreary interior can be cooked until it is voluptuous and golden, yielding and crusty, meltingly tender.

Its Chinese or Indian origins make it a natural partner to traditional Asian ingredients like spices, coconut, sesame, hoisin and black or yellow bean sauces, but it is equally at home in the Mediterranean, with olive oil, garlic, onions, coriander, mint, basil and parsley. Although its flavour is not pronounced, however you cook it, it is very distinctive and can take some fairly strong partners.

Tip: Many recipes call for aubergines to be salted and left to 'degorge' their bitter juices and thereby soak up less oil when cooking, but I have never found this necessary.

Ingredients

3 x 400g tins butter beans, drained and rinsed
3 garlic cloves, peeled
125ml and 8 tbsp olive oil
Fresh lemon juice
700g aubergines, peeled and cut into 2cm pieces
1/2 tsp each cumin, coriander and fennel seeds, toasted and coarsely ground (page 86)
4 spring onions, trimmed and finely sliced
180g cherry tomatoes, quartered
4 tbsp sun-dried tomato purée
1 tsp balsamic vinegar
10g basil, shredded
Sea salt and freshly ground black pepper

need2know

Method

1 Place the butter beans, garlic, 125ml of olive oil, 2 tbsp of lemon juice and some seasoning in a food processor and process until fairly smooth. You may need to add a bit of water to enable the blades to turn efficiently.

2 Check the seasoning and the acidity, adding some more lemon juice if it needs sparkle, but remember that the flavours will be more pronounced once it is hot, so tread lightly and check it again before serving. The purée can be refrigerated for up to 3 days.

3 To heat the purée, transfer it to a heat-proof bowl and place it over a pan of simmering water. Leave it to warm up, stirring occasionally.

4 Preheat the oven to 200°C/400°F/Gas Mark 6/fan oven 180°C.

5 Arrange the aubergine pieces in one layer in a roasting tray, drizzle with 4 tbsp of olive oil, season well and roast in the oven, stirring every so often, until they are golden and crusty, about 40 minutes.

6 When the aubergines are nearly done, gently stir the ground spice mixture into them and return to the oven for a further 5 minutes.

7 Mix the onions, tomatoes, sun-dried tomato purée, vinegar, remaining olive oil, basil and some seasoning in a small bowl.

8 Spread the butter bean purée in a wide, deep serving dish. Spoon the aubergines over it and top with the salsa.

9 Serve immediately.

Cannellini Bean Bruschetta

Serves 2 for lunch or 4 as a first course

Bruschetta started off as nothing more than a piece of toasted bread used to sample the new olive oil as it came out of the press, but sophistication has caught up with it and it has been transformed, very successfully I must say, into one of the darlings of modern Italian cooking. It makes a lovely lunch dish, particularly when eaten in the garden on a sunny day and accompanied by a glass of chilled rosé wine – but even if you make it in the middle of winter, the flavours and aromas will waft the summer straight into your kitchen.

Ingredients

4 slices good solid bread, 1cm thick
2 tbsp and 100ml olive oil
1 garlic clove, peeled
200g cherry tomatoes, halved
1 tsp agave nectar or runny honey (page 24)
1 tsp cumin seeds, toasted and coarsely ground (page 86)
75g red onions, peeled and finely chopped
1 garlic clove, peeled and crushed
1 red chilli, deseeded and finely sliced
3 prepared pickled lemon quarters (page 25)
225g tomatoes, quartered
2 x 400g tin cannellini beans, rinsed and drained
10g parsley, coarsely chopped
10g fresh coriander, coarsely chopped
Sea salt and freshly ground black pepper

Tip: Always use good dense bread like pain de campagne, sourdough or homemade wholemeal for these bruschette, as light loaves like ciabatta, French bread or ordinary supermarket sliced types do not have enough crumb to soak up the delicious juices.

Method

1   Heat the grill to high. Brush the bread slices on both sides with 1 tbsp of olive oil and grill until golden on both sides.

2   Rub the surface with the whole garlic clove and set aside.

3   Preheat the oven to 200°C/400°F/Gas Mark mark 6/fan oven 180°C.

4   Line a roasting tin with baking parchment and arrange the cherry tomato halves on it. Drizzle them first with agave then 1 tbsp of olive oil, season well, and bake for 20 to 30 minutes, until they are just starting to blacken around the edges. Set aside to cool.

5   The bread and cherry tomatoes can be prepared several hours ahead of time.

6   In a roomy salad bowl, combine the cumin, red onions, crushed garlic, chilli, pickled lemons and some seasoning.

7   Purée the 225g of tomatoes in a food processor with the remaining olive oil and some seasoning, and add it to the bowl, along with the cherry tomatoes, cannellini beans and herbs. Mix gently and check the seasoning.

8   Place the bruschette on two plates and top with the cannellini bean mixture.

9   Serve immediately.

Sicilian Aubergine Rolls

Serves 4 as a first course, 2 as a main course

The cuisine of Sicily has an extra layer of flavours and excitement: it is very Italian, with all the usual Italian ingredients, but it is also very strongly influenced by its proximity to North Africa. Saffron and cinnamon, dried fruit, fresh mint and coriander, yoghurt, oranges and lemons seem to feature widely in its traditional dishes, reminding me of Moroccan and Tunisian cooking. These rollatini are a bit fiddly to make, so don't try to rush them or you will be too frustrated to enjoy them by the time you have finished rolling them! The preparation needs to be relaxed and leisurely so that when you sit down to eat, you are open and receptive to the magic of the aromas, textures and contrasts.

Tip: Harissa is a chilli paste widely used in North African cookery. It can be purchased in some large supermarkets and delicatessens or by mail order.

Ingredients

450g aubergines – choose long narrow ones
Olive oil for brushing and 3 tbsp
1 small red and 1 small yellow pepper, about 150g each, grilled
150g onions, peeled and finely chopped
3 garlic cloves, peeled and crushed
1 red chilli, deseeded and finely chopped
50g dried apricots, diced
4 prepared pickled lemon quarters (page 25)
25g pistachios, toasted and coarsely chopped
2 tbsp capers, rinsed, squeezed dry and coarsely chopped
50g soft wholemeal breadcrumbs
1 tsp dried oregano
1/2 tsp harissa powder or paste or to taste (see tip)
250ml plain soya yoghurt, well seasoned (page 52)
10g chives, coarsely snipped with scissors
Sea salt and freshly ground black pepper

Method

1   Preheat the grill to high.

2   Top and tail the aubergines. Slice them lengthways about 1/2cm thick, discarding the end slices which are all skin. Brush with olive oil, arrange on a baking tray and grill 5cm from the heat until golden and soft. Alternatively, cook them on a ridged griddle pan.

3   Skin the peppers and dice the flesh.

4   Heat 2 tbsp olive oil in a medium frying pan, add the onions, 2 garlic cloves and chilli, and cook over medium heat, stirring every so often, until they start to brown. Stir in the apricots, pickled lemons and some seasoning, and cook for 5 minutes longer.

5   Remove from the heat and stir in the peppers, pistachios, capers, breadcrumbs, oregano and harissa.

6   Check the seasoning and heat, adding more harissa if it is not spicy enough for you – it all rather depends on the heat of the red chilli.

7   Lay the aubergine slices out on the work surface and season. Divide the stuffing between them, placing it at the wider end. Roll up towards the narrow end and transfer to a baking dish, seam side down. The rollatini can be prepared up to this point 24 hours in advance and refrigerated. Bring back to room temperature before cooking.

8   Preheat the oven to 200°C/400°F/Gas Mark 6/fan oven 180°C. Brush the rollatini with olive oil, cover with kitchen foil and bake for 15 minutes.

9   Mix the yoghurt with all but 1 tbsp of the chives and remaining garlic and olive oil.

10 Remove the foil from the aubergines and sprinkle with the remaining chives.

11 Serve immediately with the yoghurt.

Wrinkled Potatoes

Serves 2 as a lunch dish with a salad

'Papas arrugadas', wrinkled potatoes, are a speciality of the Canary Islands. Fresh water was a scarce commodity on these Spanish islands off the coast of Africa and the potatoes are historically cooked in sea water, which shrivels them and wrinkles the skin and gives them a wonderfully savoury (and obviously salty!) flavour. They are traditionally served with two fresh, spicy, very garlicky sauces, known as 'mojos': red mojo or Mojo Rojo is based on red peppers and tomatoes, while green mojo or Mojo Verde is bright with fresh coriander.

Ingredients

1 kg small new potatoes (ideally the size of a walnut), scrubbed
500g coarse sea salt
2 tbsp and 125ml and 200ml olive oil
1 medium red pepper, about 150g, grilled
2 garlic cloves, peeled
2 tsp cumin seeds, toasted and medium ground (page 86)
125g tomatoes, quartered
1/2 tsp hot smoked paprika (pimentón picante) (see tip on page 40)
1 tbsp sherry or red wine vinegar
80g fresh coriander
1 hottish green chilli, deseeded and coarsely chopped
1 tbsp fresh lemon juice
Sea salt and freshly ground black pepper

Method

1 Place the potatoes in a saucepan and add the coarse salt and enough water to cover. Bring to the boil and simmer until tender, about 15 minutes. Drain and return to the pan with 2 tbsp of olive oil. Stir well to coat.

2 Make the two mojos while the potatoes are cooking. Skin the pepper and chop the flesh coarsely. Place in a food processor with 125ml of olive oil, 1 garlic clove, half the cumin, the paprika, vinegar and some seasoning and blend until smooth. Taste and adjust the seasoning.

3 Rinse out the bowl of the food processor. Place the remaining olive oil, garlic and cumin in it, along with the coriander, chilli, lemon juice and some seasoning, and blend until smooth. Taste and adjust the seasoning.

Tip: Salt comes in many shapes and forms nowadays, from pink and black Himalayan salt through Fleur de Sel down to plain table salt. They vary widely in quality and flavour, and many salts contain additives to stop them from caking and make them flow freely. The Geo brand of fine and coarse sea salts is excellent and available in most large supermarkets or from The Ethical Superstore.

4   Grind some black pepper into the potatoes and shake them around gently.

5   Serve immediately with the mojos.

Spaghetti with Avocado Salsa

Serves 4

This Mexican inspired salsa for pasta can pretty much be put together in the time it takes to cook some wholemeal spaghetti, making it a perfect dish for a weekday evening – all that is required is some slicing, chopping, toasting and grinding. And as the ingredients are all raw, the flavours are sparkling and bright. The overall heat is up to you: you can use a fiery or mild chilli, or even leave it out – and the sprinkle of chipotle is optional.

Ingredients

1 tbsp each cumin and coriander seeds, toasted, coarsely ground (page 86)
225g cherry tomatoes, quartered – a mixture of red and yellow looks pretty
1 red chilli, deseeded and finely sliced
50g red onions, peeled and finely chopped
2 garlic cloves, peeled and crushed
1/2 lime, juiced
2 large ripe avocadoes, peeled and diced
4 tbsp olive oil
25g fresh coriander, coarsely chopped
350g wholemeal spaghetti
1 tsp chipotle chilli powder or to taste (page 29)
Sea salt and freshly ground black pepper

Method

1   In a large bowl, mix the spices, cherry tomatoes, chilli, onions, garlic and lime juice. Carefully fold in the avocadoes, oil, coriander and some seasoning.

2   Cook the spaghetti according to the manufacturer's instructions and drain well. Divide between four warm plates and top with the salsa.

3   Sprinkle with chipotle powder and serve immediately.

Tip: The rich, creamy texture of avocadoes is just one of their assets. They are nutritional power houses, packed with minerals, phytonutrients, protein and essential fatty acids.

Carrot Cakes with Cucumber and Coriander Raita

Serves 4 as a first course, 2 as a main course

Rich with curry spices and bright with chilli, these Indian-inspired pancakes are reminiscent of bhajis, with a crisp outer coating and a tender interior, but unlike traditional bhajis which are deep-fried and often rather heavy and indigestible, these are merely cooked in a bit of olive oil, making them light and infinitely healthier.

Ingredients

100g chickpea flour (page 60)
1/2 tsp baking powder
1 tbsp ground cumin
5 tsp ground coriander
1 tsp ground turmeric
1 1/2 tsp salt
2 hottish red chillies, deseeded and finely sliced
150g carrots, scrubbed and coarsely grated
6 spring onions, trimmed and finely sliced
25g fresh coriander, coarsely chopped
75g cucumber, deseeded and diced
1 garlic clove, peeled
250ml plain soya yoghurt (page 52)
2 tbsp toasted sesame oil
Fresh lime juice
Olive oil
Sea salt and freshly ground black pepper

Tip: It is important to use chillies with plenty of fire to them, as cooked carrots can be a bit lacklustre and tend to benefit from some sizzle. If, however, you are not a fire-eater, increase the ground cumin and coriander to ensure that the pancakes are boldly flavoured.

Method

1. Sift the flour with the baking powder, cumin, 4 tsp of ground coriander, turmeric and salt into a mixing bowl and stir in just enough cold water to make a very thick batter.

2. Add one red chilli, the carrots, onions and half the fresh coriander and set aside.

3. For the raita, combine the remaining ground and fresh coriander, chilli, cucumber, garlic, yoghurt, sesame oil, about 1 tbsp fresh lime juice and some pepper in a small bowl. Add some salt just before serving, and a bit more lime juice if it is in the least bit bland.

4. Preheat the oven to its lowest setting and put a plate in to warm.

5. Heat some olive oil in a heavy non-stick frying pan over medium heat.

6. Drop large spoonfuls – as close to 1/8th as you can! – into the pan and flatten them slightly with a spatula.

7. Lower the heat and cook for about 4 minutes, until you can see that the pancakes are starting to turn golden around the edges. Carefully flip them over and cook the other side for about 2 minutes. You want the carrot to be cooked but the pancake to remain moist.

8. Remove the pancakes to the plate in the oven to keep warm and cook the remaining batter in the same way.

9. Transfer the pancakes to warm plates, top with a good spoonful of raita and serve immediately.

Stuffed Vine Leaves

Serves 4

A dish calculated to bring back memories of white sand beaches, waterside tavernas and blazing sunshine! It takes time to fill and roll the leaves, so do not be tempted to embark on the whole procedure on a weekday evening when you have had a challenging journey home from work – keep this recipe for a weekend when you can benefit from its therapeutic preparation.

Ingredients

Tip: If any of the vine leaves are a bit small or have holes, use other small or torn leaves to extend or patch them.

200g onions, peeled and coarsely chopped
175g brown basmati rice
100g roasted, chopped hazelnuts
1 x 400g tin chopped tomatoes
Grated rind of 2 lemons
2 tsp bouillon powder
70g dried apricots, diced
2 tsp sea salt
250g vine leaves in brine, well rinsed, stalks removed
80ml olive oil
750ml water
Freshly ground black pepper

Method

1 Mix the first eight ingredients in a bowl.

2 Lay out 4 or 5 vine leaves on the work surface, smooth side down. Place a good tablespoon of stuffing in the middle and fold first the base and then the left side of the leaf up and over the rice. Now fold the right side of the leaf up and over and roll the leaf away from you into a neat cylinder, firmly but not too tightly as the rice will expand as it cooks. Arrange the filled leaves in the bottom of a medium saucepan, packing them in snugly.

3 Repeat the procedure with the remaining leaves and stuffing.

4 Pour the olive oil and water into the saucepan, cover and bring to the boil over medium heat. Turn the heat right down and simmer for 1 hour and 15 minutes.

5 The vine leaves can be served warm or at room temperature, and keep well in the refrigerator for up to 5 days.

Caramelised Onion Pissaladière

Serves 4 generously

Pissaladière is one of the glories of southern French cuisine, a thin crust topped with onions, anchovies and olives, made in the boulangeries early in the morning and cut into large squares. Pastry – either puff or shortcrust – is often used but a yeasted bread dough is more traditional, as well as easier and more satisfying to make.

Ingredients

300g wholemeal bread flour
5g dried yeast
1 1/2 tsp sea salt
1 tsp sugar
4 tbsp olive oil
200ml warm water
1.4 kg onions, peeled and sliced
15g fresh thyme, leaves stripped from the stalks and coarsely chopped
16 cherry tomatoes, halved
15 pitted black olives, halved
Sea salt and freshly ground black pepper

Method

1   In a large bowl, mix the flour, yeast, salt, sugar and 1 tbsp of olive oil. Add the water, stir everything together with a large wooden spoon until it forms a ball and turn the dough out onto the work surface. Knead until smooth and elastic, about 10 minutes, adding a bit more flour if it is sticky. Place in a lightly greased bowl and cover with a damp dishcloth. Set aside in a warm place until it has doubled in size, about an hour.

2   While the dough is rising, heat the remaining olive oil in a large frying pan, add the onions and plenty of seasoning, and cook over medium heat, stirring often, until they start to turn golden. Stir in the thyme and check the seasoning.

3   Preheat the oven to 200°C/400°F/Gas Mark mark 6/fan oven 180°C.

4   Roll the dough out as thinly as possible on a large sheet of baking parchment or silicone oven sheet. Lift it carefully onto a baking tray and spread with the onions, leaving a 2cm border all the way round. Sprinkle with tomatoes and olives.

5   Bake in the oven for 45 minutes, until the crust is crisp.

6   Serve immediately although it is very good cold.

Tip: The onions take time to peel and slice but they can be prepared the day before and stored in a freezer bag in the fridge - seal the bag tightly though or the smell will seep out and permeate everything else.

Spinach And Ricotta Pancakes

Serves 4

The darling of the Italian trattoria goes vegan: chickpea flour in the pancakes and nut cheese instead of ricotta. The filling is spiked with fresh oregano and the accompanying roasted tomato sauce adds plenty of acidity to balance any richness. The pancakes, spinach mixture and sauce can all be made well ahead of time and the dish can be assembled in minutes before baking.

Tip: Pancakes made with chickpea flour tend to dry out quite quickly so if you are not using them immediately, place them in a freezer bag until required.

Ingredients

250g chickpea flour (page 60)
2 tbsp olive oil and extra for frying
150g onions, peeled and finely chopped
2 garlic cloves, peeled and crushed
550g baby leaf spinach, well washed and drained
15g fresh oregano, leaves only, coarsely chopped
Whole nutmeg
1 x quantity nut cheese made with cashews (page 87)
1 x quantity Roasted Tomato Sauce (page 24), heated
Sea salt and freshly ground black pepper

Method

1. Place the flour in a bowl and whisk in 300ml cold water and 1 tsp of salt. Set aside while you prepare the filling.

2. Heat 2 tbsp of oil in a frying pan and stir in the onions and garlic. Turn the heat right down and leave to cook gently until they start to turn golden.

3. Cook the spinach in a large frying pan over high heat until it is wilted. Transfer it to a colander and press out all the moisture with a wooden spoon. Cool slightly then chop coarsely. Add to the onions along with the oregano, a good scraping of nutmeg and the nut cheese. Check the seasoning.

4. Brush a 15cm non-stick frying pan with oil and pour in just enough chickpea batter to cover the bottom, twirling the pan to spread it out thinly. Cook for about 2 minutes, until pale gold, then flip over and cook the other side in the same way.

5. When all the pancakes are cooked, lay them out on the work surface and divide the filling between them. Roll them up and place them in an ovenproof dish where they fit snugly. Cover the dish tightly with foil.

6 Preheat the oven to 200°C/400°F/Gas Mark 6/fan oven 180°C and bake the pancakes for 30 minutes. Remove the foil and pour over the tomato sauce.

7 Serve immediately.

Quesadillas with Salsa Verde

Serves 2

Quesadillas are tortilla turnovers, which are traditionally filled with cheese and any other ingredient which takes the cook's fancy, and lightly fried on both sides to form a crisp, crunchy, golden envelope. In this recipe, I am using a nut 'cheese' made with pine nuts and spiked with sun-dried tomato purée.

Ingredients

30g flat leaf parsley
1 garlic clove, peeled
1 tbsp capers, rinsed and squeezed dry
1 tsp bouillon powder
1 tsp smooth Dijon mustard
2 fat spring onions, trimmed and coarsely sliced
15 pitted green olives
120ml olive oil and extra for frying
1 tbsp sun-dried tomato purée
1 x quantity nut cheese made with pine nuts (page 87)
2 x 15cm corn tortillas (see tip)
125g plum cherry tomatoes, quartered
Sea salt and freshly ground black pepper

Method

1 Process the first eight ingredients and some seasoning until you have a slightly chunky sauce. Scrape into a bowl and set aside while you make the quesadillas.

2 Stir the tomato purée into the nut cheese and check the seasoning.

3 Brush a non-stick frying pan with a bit of olive oil and place it over medium heat.

4 Lay the two tortillas out on the work surface and spread the nut cheese over one half of each tortilla. Fold them over into a half-moon shape and press down lightly. Cook them in the frying pan for about 4 minutes on each side, until they are crisp and golden.

5 Stir the cherry tomatoes into the salsa verde.

6 Transfer the quesadillas to two warm plates and top with a spoonful of the salsa.

7 Serve immediately with the remaining salsa on the side.

Tip: Tortillas are thin corn pancakes traditional to Mexican cuisine. Widely available in the world foods sections of supermarkets, they vary in quality and size. The most popular brand is Old El Paso but they are very sweet. Discovery corn tortillas are considerably better and authentic. Mexican corn tortillas are available by mail order.

7

Chilli and Spice – Warmth and Seasoning

Dynamite in the kitchen! Where would most modern world cuisines be without fiery chillies, lemony coriander seeds, bright yellow turmeric, fragrant black peppercorns and refreshing ginger, to name but a few? Across the globe, chillies and a myriad of spices appear in indigenous and regional dishes, imparting warmth and fragrance, fascination, flavour and basic seasoning.

While chillies came from the New World and therefore only started appearing in international cuisine from the 16th century onwards, spices have been an important constituent of the human larder for much longer and spread across the world along the ancient historical spice routes. They were an extremely valuable commodity, on a par with gold and silver, and had numerous uses beyond the kitchen: cinnamon, anise and cumin, for instance, were used by the Egyptians to embalm the dead, and Chinese medicine draws extensively on spices for many of its remedies.

Chillies and spices come in various forms and are used in different ways:

- Chillies can be fresh, dried and powdered, as well as incorporated into prepared sauces like sweet chilli sauce and Tabasco.

- Fresh chillies vary in heat, from mild green jalapeños to mind-bendingly hot Scotch bonnets, and since this degree of heat can make a surprising different in a dish, I have specified in the recipes when a properly hot chilli is required.

- Whole spices are infinitely more aromatic than their ground counterparts and keep well, so be sure to have a good stock to hand. I have to admit, however, that ground cumin and coriander, for instance, can be very practical on occasions and I do avail myself of them from time to time. Nevertheless, they lose their flavour and aroma quickly so they are only a standby!

- Spice mixtures like ras el hanout, garam masala and curry pastes are time-consuming to make, as well as frustrating since one seldom uses more than a spoonful or so and the remainder languishes in the store cupboard or refrigerator while its charms rapidly diminish. I therefore buy them ready-made and replace them often.

- Heat brings out the talents of most spices and toasting them whole before adding them to other food does wonders (see below).

- To flavour a liquid, place it in a saucepan, add the whole spice and heat slowly until steaming. Remove from the heat and set aside until cool. Strain to remove the spice. This method works particularly well with spices like cloves, cinnamon quills, vanilla, star anise and cardamom pods.

To toast whole spices

Method

Place the spices in a heavy frying pan, without oil or moisture, and stir-fry them over medium heat until they start to smell nutty and aromatic. Remove immediately from the heat and transfer to a mortar or electric spice grinder and grind to the desired consistency. Use this method for cumin, coriander, cloves and pepper. Care must be taken not to brown them too thoroughly as this can make them bitter.

Roasted Aubergines with Satay Sauce

Serves 2 as a side dish or snack

This is a wonderfully easy dish which takes time to cook but only minutes to prepare, and the sesame oil and sauce give a tremendous lift to what can be a rather bland, uninteresting vegetable. Aubergines are spongy and absorb other flavours easily, so the more often you brush it with oil while it is in the oven, the more nutty its flavour will become.

Ingredients

1 large aubergine, about 375g
Toasted sesame oil for brushing and 1 tbsp
1 garlic clove, peeled
50g smooth peanut butter
2 tsp tamarind paste (see tip on page 150)
2 tsp Madras curry paste
4 slices pickled ginger (see tip)
250ml plain soya yoghurt
10g fresh tarragon, coarsely chopped
1 hot red chilli, deseeded and finely sliced
Sea salt and freshly ground black pepper

Method

1   Preheat the oven to 200°C/400°F/Gas Mark 6/fan oven 180°C.

2   Cut off the aubergine stem and quarter the aubergine lengthways. Place on a baking tray, skin side down, brush generously with sesame oil and season. Bake for about 45 minutes, until soft and golden, brushing again with oil two or three times as it cooks.

3   Make the satay sauce by blending 1 tbsp of sesame oil, the garlic, peanut butter, tamarind and curry pastes, ginger and yoghurt with some salt in a food processor. Check the seasoning.

4   When the aubergines are ready, transfer them to a warm serving dish, spoon the sauce over them and sprinkle with tarragon and chilli.

5   Serve immediately.

Tip: In Japan, paper-thin slices of ginger are pickled in vinegar to make a condiment known as 'gari' which traditionally accompanies sushi. It has a lovely sweet and sharp, pungent and cleansing flavour and is an excellent way to add a bit of kick to a salsa or dressing. Clearspring is a good brand and is available in most large supermarkets and delicatessens.

Sweet Potato, Aubergine and Tamarind Soup

Serves 4

This is a soup for a cold winter's night, caramelised, rib-sticking, satisfying and spicy. The curry paste cuts through the sweetness of the potato but if you are not a spice lover, you can use a milder curry paste. However, some warmth and spiciness is essential – I have tried using just cumin and coriander seeds for instance, and found that their flavour is totally eclipsed by the sweet potato.

Ingredients

6 tbsp toasted sesame oil, plus extra for drizzling
550g aubergines, peeled and diced
550g sweet potatoes, peeled and cut into 1cm pieces
375g red onions, peeled and coarsely chopped
4 garlic cloves, peeled and coarsely chopped
3 tbsp Madras curry paste or to taste
1 tbsp each cumin and coriander seeds, toasted and finely ground (page 86)
1 tsp bouillon powder
450ml water
3 tbsp tamarind paste (see tip)
2 tbsp dark tahini (page 109)
2 fat spring onions, trimmed and finely sliced
10g fresh chives, coarsely snipped with scissors
Sea salt and freshly ground black pepper

Method

1   Heat 3 tbsp of the sesame oil in a large frying pan, add the diced aubergines and cook, stirring often, until nicely browned. Set aside.

2   While the aubergines are cooking, heat 3 tbsp of oil in a saucepan, add the sweet potatoes, red onions and garlic, and cook over medium heat, stirring every now and then, until soft and golden. Stir in the curry paste, spices, bouillon powder and some seasoning, and cook for a further 5 minutes.

3   Add the water and tamarind paste, bring to the boil, cover the pan, turn the heat right down and simmer for 30 minutes.

4   Cool slightly and blend in a food processor with the tahini until smooth. Return to the pan, stir in the aubergines, reheat gently and check the seasoning.

Tip: Tamarind paste is available in jars in the spice section of most supermarkets. Its sweet and sour citrusy flavour is common in Asian cooking and it can be used in many cases instead of lemon juice to counteract blandness. Its sharpness works well with other sweetish vegetables like pumpkin, courgettes and onions.

5 Mix the spring onions and chives in a small bowl.

6 Ladle the soup into four warm bowls and sprinkle generously with the onions and chives.

7 Drizzle with sesame oil and serve immediately.

Bombay Baked Potatoes

Serves 2 for lunch with a salad, 4 as a side dish

While plain baked potatoes with plenty of fruity olive oil are hard to beat, scooping out the flesh and mashing it with various seasonings lifts them to new heights. Although they do take a certain amount of preparation, once stuffed the potatoes can be left for several hours or even overnight in the refrigerator, and given a second baking at your convenience.

Tip: Rubbing the potato skin with olive oil and salt hardens it slightly and makes it less liable to tear and split when you are scooping out the flesh.

Ingredients

3 baking potatoes, about 300g each
2 tbsp olive oil
8 garlic cloves, peeled
50g ginger, peeled and coarsely chopped
2 red chillies, as hot as you like
150g onions, peeled and chopped
75g coconut cream, coarsely chopped
1 tbsp cumin seeds, toasted and coarsely ground (page 86)
1/2 tsp ground turmeric
10g parsley, coarsely chopped
25g fresh coriander, coarsely chopped
1 tbsp tamarind paste (page 150)
250ml plain soya yoghurt
1 garlic clove, peeled and crushed
100g roasted cashew nuts, coarsely chopped
Sea salt and freshly ground black pepper

Method

1 Preheat the oven to 200°C/400°F/Gas Mark 6/fan oven 180°C.

2 Prick the potatoes in several places with the tip of a knife, rub them with 1 tbsp of olive oil and salt, and bake until fairly soft, about an hour and a quarter.

3 Set aside until cool enough to handle, then carefully cut in half lengthways. Scoop out the flesh with a teaspoon, place in a bowl and mash.

4 While the potatoes are cooking, purée the 8 garlic cloves, ginger, chillies, onions, coconut cream, spices, parsley, half the coriander, tamarind and 1 1/2 tsp of salt in a food processor until fairly finely chopped.

5 Add the mixture to the mashed potatoes and mix well with a fork.

6 Pile the mixture back into 4 of the potato skins – eat the other 2 as cook's perks, sprinkled with salt and dipped in olive oil!

7 The stuffed potatoes can be prepared up to this point and refrigerated overnight; bring them back to room temperature before their final bake.

8 Preheat the oven to 200°C/400°F/Gas Mark 6/fan oven 180°C and bake the potatoes for 30 minutes.

9 While the potatoes are cooking, mix the yoghurt with 1 tbsp of olive oil, the crushed garlic, remaining coriander and plenty of seasoning. Stir in the cashews shortly before serving.

10 Serve the potatoes with the yoghurt.

Chickpea and Fruit Curry with Herbed Chatni

Serves 4

Deeply savoury stews and casseroles are one of the delights of vegan cuisine. They are infinitely varied and flexible, showcasing the properties of just one specific vegetable or a combination of many. In this case, the chickpeas add body and protein, the coconut and fruit a welcome sweetness to offset the spices, and the chatni texture, heat and aromatic herbiness.

Ingredients

1 large aubergine, about 300g, peeled and cut into 1cm cubes
300g sweet potato, peeled and cut into 1cm cubes
3 tbsp coconut or olive oil (page 164)
150g onions, peeled and coarsely chopped
3 garlic cloves, peeled and crushed
40g fresh ginger, peeled and finely chopped
1/4 tsp ground turmeric
6 green cardamom pods
1 tsp cumin seeds, toasted and medium ground (page 86)
1 tbsp coriander seeds, toasted and medium ground (page 86)
1/2 tsp fennel seeds, toasted and medium ground (page 86)
1 tbsp Madras curry paste
1 x 400g tin chopped tomatoes
1 x 400g tin coconut milk
1 x 400g tin chickpeas, drained and rinsed
1 large, slightly unripe banana, sliced into 1/2cm rounds
2 tbsp olive oil
1 red and 1 green chilli, deseeded and finely chopped
15g fresh coriander, coarsely chopped
50g red onions, peeled and finely chopped
25g raisins, soaked in boiling water for 30 minutes and squeezed dry
1 tbsp fresh lime juice
100g roasted peanuts
Sea salt and freshly ground black pepper
Rice or Indian breads, to serve (optional)

Tip: While the English word 'chutney' is thought to be derived from 'chatni', the Hindi for a blend of spices and vegetables or fruit which accompany a main dish and tone down its overall heat, a chutney is normally fruit cooked to a pulp with vinegar and sugar and aimed more at the Western world than the Indian sub-continent. I therefore prefer to use 'chatni', which describes the accompaniment to this curry far more accurately.

Method

1 Preheat the oven to 200°C/400°F/Gas Mark 6/fan oven 180°C.

2 Place the aubergines and sweet potatoes in a baking dish, drizzle with 2 tbsp of oil, season well and roast in the oven, stirring occasionally, for one hour, until soft and blackening along the edges.

3 In the meantime, heat another tablespoon of oil in a medium saucepan, add the onions, 2 garlic cloves and ginger, and cook gently, stirring often, until soft and golden. Sprinkle in all the spices and the curry paste and stir-fry for a minute.

4 Add the tomatoes, coconut milk and chickpeas, turn the heat down to low, and leave to simmer for 30 minutes.

5 When the aubergines and sweet potatoes are ready, stir them into the curry along with the banana and cook for a further 10 minutes. Check the seasoning.

6 For the chatni, mix the 2 tbsp of olive oil, remaining garlic clove, chillies, coriander, red onions, raisins and lime juice in a small bowl. Stir in the peanuts just before serving.

7 Spoon the curry into a warm serving dish and sprinkle some of the chatni over the top.

8 Serve immediately with rice or Indian breads and the remaining chatni on the side.

Warm Spiced Potato Salad

Serves 4

A potato salad with a difference – the difference being a good spoonful of Mexican chipotle chilli paste, with its mellow heat and smokiness. But the chilli is not the only Mexican ingredient: potatoes, avocadoes and tomatoes all originated in the New World, and although cumin and coriander were brought to the Americas by immigrants and settlers, they are two very typical Mexican flavours.

Tip: The pale green flesh of the avocado turns black very quickly when exposed to oxygen so it is always better to peel and prepare it at the last moment.

Ingredients

700g potatoes, scrubbed
3 tbsp olive oil
1 tbsp cumin seeds, toasted and finely ground (page 86)
4 fat spring onions, trimmed and finely sliced
1 garlic clove, peeled and crushed
1 hottish red chilli, seeded and finely sliced
1 tbsp chipotle chilli paste (page 29)
1 heaped tsp dried oregano, preferably Mexican
200g cherry tomatoes, quartered
2 ripe avocadoes
10g basil, shredded
Sea salt and freshly ground black pepper

Method

1. Preheat the oven to 200°C/400°F/Gas Mark 6/fan oven 180°C and bring a large saucepan of water to the boil.

2. Cut the potatoes into wedges about the size of your thumb and boil them for 5 minutes. Drain well and place in a roasting stray. Drizzle with 1 tbsp of the olive oil, season and roast, stirring occasionally, until golden and crusty, about 45 minutes.

3. When the potatoes are almost ready, place the remaining olive oil, cumin, onions, garlic, red chilli, chipotle, oregano, tomatoes and some seasoning in a roomy bowl and mix thoroughly but gently. Fold in the potatoes and coriander.

4. Cut the avocadoes in half and, with a teaspoon, remove the flesh and sprinkle it over the potatoes. Give it all one last, very light stir.

5. Serve immediately.

Tofu Scramble

Serves 2

'Migas', meaning breadcrumbs, is the peculiar name used to describe a Mexican dish of spicy scrambled eggs garnished with tortilla strips. It is rich, mellow and satisfying, with the crisp tortillas providing an excellent contrast to the overall softness of the rest of the dish. Tofu scrambles to an equally good consistency, and using tortilla chips, rather than having to cut tortillas into strips and fry them, makes the whole dish quick and easy.

Tip: If you are not a chilli lover, omit the fresh chillies and chipotle and add 1 tbsp of sun-dried tomato purée to the tomatoes - which will make it more Italian than Mexican!

Ingredients

2 tbsp olive oil
175g onions, peeled and coarsely chopped
1 garlic clove, peeled and crushed
1 hottish red chilli, deseeded and finely sliced
1 heaped tsp cumin seeds, toasted and medium ground (page 86)
1/2 tsp chipotle chilli paste or powder or to taste (page 29)
1 tsp fine sea salt
1 tsp bouillon powder
200g tomatoes, coarsely chopped
250g firm tofu, drained and very coarsely mashed
65g plain tortilla chips
10g fresh coriander, coarsely chopped
Freshly ground black pepper

Method

1   Heat the olive oil in a heavy frying pan, add the onions, garlic and chilli, and cook over medium heat, stirring regularly, until they start to brown.

2   Sprinkle in the cumin, chipotle, salt and bouillon powder and grind in some black pepper.

3   Stir-fry for a minute or two before adding the tomatoes and cook briskly for five minutes to evaporate some of their moisture.

4   Stir in the tofu and cook the mixture until it has heated through.

5   Fold in the tortilla chips and sprinkle with coriander.

6   Serve immediately.

Onion Bhaji Pancakes with Cucumber and Pomegranate Salad

Makes 6 pancakes

Legend has it that the onion bhaji was born in the textile mills of Mumbai, and was developed to provide the workers with a quick and light lunchtime snack which would not knock them out for the rest of the afternoon. Whatever its origins, it is now a favourite street food in India and probably appears on the menu of each and every Indian restaurant worldwide.

Ingredients

100g chickpea flour (page 60)
1/2 tsp ground turmeric
1 heaped tsp cumin seeds, toasted and medium ground (page 86)
1/2 tsp baking powder
1 tsp fine sea salt
150g onions, peeled and thinly sliced
1 red and 1 green chilli, deseeded and finely sliced
50g fresh coriander, coarsely chopped
25g red onions, peeled and finely chopped
25g fresh mint, coarsely chopped
Seeds from 1 small pomegranate (page 62)
1 garlic clove, peeled and crushed
1 lime, grated zest and juice
100g cucumber, deseeded and diced
3 tbsp olive oil and extra for frying
250ml plain soya yoghurt
1 tbsp pomegranate molasses (page 94)
1 lime, juiced
Sea salt and freshly ground black pepper

Tip: The traditional cooking technique for bhajis is deep-frying, but since this particular method is banned from my kitchen on health grounds, I have transformed the bhaji into a pancake which can be cooked with a minimum amount of olive oil.

Method

1 Sift the flour, spices, baking powder and salt into a mixing bowl and add just enough cold water to make a very thick batter.

2 Stir in the sliced onions, chillies and half the coriander, and set aside to rest.

3 For the salad, combine the red onions, remaining coriander, half the mint, pomegranate, garlic, juice and zest of one lime, cucumber and 2 tbsp of olive oil in a bowl. Season just before serving.

4 Mix together the yoghurt, molasses, juice of one lime, remaining mint, 1 tbsp of olive oil and some seasoning.

5 Preheat the oven to its lowest setting and put a plate in to warm.

6 Heat some olive oil in a heavy non-stick frying pan over medium heat. Drop large spoonfuls – as close to 1/6th as you can! – into the pan and flatten them slightly with a spatula.

7 Lower the heat and cook for about four minutes, until you can see that the pancakes are starting to turn golden around the edges. Carefully flip them over and cook the other side for about two minutes. You want the onions to be cooked but the pancake to remain moist.

8 Remove the pancakes to the plate in the oven to keep warm and cook the remaining batter in the same way.

9 Transfer the pancakes to warm plates, drizzle them with yoghurt, and serve immediately with the salad.

Thai Green Curry

Serves 2 as a main course

This is a straightforward curry, with basic seasonings of onions, garlic and fresh ginger, a good kick of Thai green curry paste to give it some depth, and plenty of coconut milk. The magic ingredient is the tamarind, with its mouth-puckering sparkle, which cuts straight through the opulent sweetness of the coconut, cools the heat and brings a welcome sharp balance to the whole dish.

Ingredients

3 tbsp toasted sesame oil
200g onions, peeled and coarsely chopped
2 garlic cloves, peeled and crushed
50g fresh ginger, peeled and finely chopped or grated
1/2 tsp ground turmeric
1 tbsp Thai green curry paste, or to taste
1 to 2 tbsp tamarind paste (see tip on page 150)
400ml coconut milk
50g solid coconut cream, coarsely chopped (see tip on page 116)
100g frozen petits pois, defrosted
100g French beans, topped, tailed, halved and cooked
100g sugarsnap peas, trimmed and cooked
50g frozen leaf spinach, defrosted
10g Thai basil or tarragon, coarsely chopped
1 large red and 1 large green chilli, deseeded and finely sliced
100g pumpkin seeds, toasted (page 86)
Sea salt and freshly ground black pepper
Cooked rice, to serve (optional)

Tip: While I have used green vegetables in this curry, feel free to substitute any others which take your fancy or you have to hand: carrots, potatoes, parsnips and swedes, asparagus, Brussels sprouts, okra, courgettes and aubergines all work well.

Method

1 Heat the oil in a heavy frying pan, add the onions, garlic and ginger, and cook over medium heat, stirring regularly, until they start to brown. Add the turmeric, curry paste, one tbsp of tamarind and some seasoning and cook for a further two minutes.

2 Pour in the coconut milk, turn the heat right down, and leave it all to reduce until the sauce is rich and thick. Stir in the coconut cream and let it melt.

3 Add the green vegetables and check the seasoning – if it tastes a bit flat, add some more tamarind to sharpen it and balance the flavours – some brands of coconut milk can be quite sweet.

4 Sprinkle with basil, chillies and pumpkin seeds and serve immediately with rice.

Spiced Moroccan Chickpeas

Serves 2

Tip: Ras el hanout, which translates bizarrely as 'head of the shop', is a popular North African spice blend and the particular combination of spices seems to depend on whatever the spice seller fancies. I have even found rose petals in it. It is available in most supermarkets or by mail order.

Native to the Middle East, chickpeas feature extensively in the modern ethnic cuisines of the area, from the Lebanese hummus to Moroccan tagines and soups like harira, used to break the Ramadan fast. This is a quick and easy dish, dry rather than stewy, and flavoured with that very Moroccan spice mixture called ras el hanout (see tip).

Ingredients

2 tbsp olive oil
175g onions, peeled and coarsely chopped
2 garlic cloves, peeled and crushed
1 1/2 tsp ras el hanout
1/2 tsp ground turmeric
300g tomatoes, coarsely chopped
50g raisins
1 x 400g tin chickpeas, rinsed
2 prepared pickled lemon quarters (page 25)
Fresh lemon juice
10g flat leaf parsley, coarsely chopped
Sea salt and freshly ground black pepper

Method

1   Heat the olive oil in a heavy frying pan, add the onions and garlic, and cook over medium heat, stirring occasionally, until they start to brown, about 10 minutes.

2   Stir in the ras el hanout and turmeric and cook for a further two minutes, then add the tomatoes and raisins. Continue to cook for five minutes, by which time the tomatoes will have started to release their moisture.

3   Add the chickpeas, pickled lemons and some seasoning, and squeeze in about 1 tbsp of fresh lemon juice.

4   Stir until the mixture is steaming and check the seasoning and acidity – depending on their sweetness, the raisins can make the whole dish a bit cloying so use more lemon juice if necessary to balance the flavours.

5   Sprinkle with parsley and serve immediately.

Red Chilaquiles with Yoghurt and Avocado

Serves 2

Chilaquiles are almost an institution in Mexico, drawn from poverty cooking and, at their simplest, consist of nothing more than a handful of stale tortillas moistened with a bit of tomato sauce. They are served mainly at breakfast, probably as a good way to use up yesterday's leftover tortillas! I tend to cheat and use tortilla chips instead as unused tortillas do not hang around my kitchen and invariably go straight into the freezer.

Ingredients

1 x quantity Roasted Tomato Sauce (page 24)
150g plain tortilla chips
10g fresh coriander, coarsely chopped
1 large red chilli, deseeded and finely sliced
1 small, ripe avocado, peeled, stoned and diced
Plain soya yoghurt, well seasoned (page 52)
Sea salt and freshly ground black pepper

Method

1   Heat the tomato sauce to steaming and pour in just enough water to make it a soupy consistency – the tortillas will absorb the moisture. Check the seasoning, leaving it slightly on the bland side as tortilla chips are salty.

2   With a large kitchen spoon, fold in the tortilla chips, turning them over and over in the sauce until they are well coated.

3   Divide the chilaquiles between two warm plates and sprinkle with coriander, chilli and avocado.

4   Drizzle with yoghurt and serve immediately.

Tip: If you love spicy food, feel free to add some kick to the sauce with chilli flakes or chipotle chilli powder, or simply use more or hotter chillies in the topping.

Hot Sweet Coconut Dahl

Serves 4

Tip: Coconut oil is a very stable cooking oil which does not burn easily. It is available from many supermarkets and health shops, as well as Ethical Superstore, and adds an extra layer of richness to the dish, but if you have none in stock, olive oil is an excellent substitute.

This Indian-inspired lentil purée is ready in half an hour, and the aromatic herby topping is easily made while the lentils cook and provides plenty of texture and vivacity. If you like a bit of heat and spice, use Madras curry paste; tikka or korma curry paste will produce a gentle, mellow dahl. Indian breads such as naan and poori are a delicious accompaniment, as is basmati rice if you prefer.

Ingredients

2 tbsp coconut or olive oil (see tip)
200g onions, peeled and coarsely chopped
1 red and 1 green chilli, deseeded and finely sliced
50g fresh ginger, peeled and coarsely chopped
3 garlic cloves, peeled and crushed
1/2 lemon, scrubbed and coarsely chopped
2 tbsp curry paste (see above)
1 tbsp whole green cardamoms
200g split red lentils, rinsed
100g solid coconut cream, coarsely chopped (see tip on page 116)
30g pine nuts, toasted (page 86)
Seeds from 1 small pomegranate
100g red onions, peeled and finely chopped
1 tbsp coriander seeds, toasted and coarsely ground
2 tbsp olive oil
1 tbsp fresh lime juice
1 tsp pomegranate molasses (see tip on page 73)
15g fresh mint, coarsely chopped
Sea salt and freshly ground black pepper

Method

1. Heat the coconut oil in a heavy saucepan and add the onions, chillies, ginger and 2 garlic cloves. Cook over medium heat, stirring occasionally, until they are softened.

2. Add the chopped lemon, curry paste and cardamom pods, and cook for a further 2 or 3 minutes.

3. Stir in the lentils and enough water to cover them by 3cm and bring to the boil. Turn the heat right down, cover the pan and simmer until the lentils have broken down and you have a thick, soft purée – about 40 minutes.

4. Add the coconut cream and some salt and pepper, and stir until the coconut has melted. Check the seasoning.

5. When the lentils are ready, assemble the topping by mixing all the remaining ingredients in a bowl and stirring in some seasoning.

6. Ladle the dahl into two warm bowls, spoon the topping over it and serve immediately.

Sweetcorn in Chilli and Chocolate Sauce

Serves 4

The notorious Mexican chilli and chocolate sauce is known as 'Mole', which simply means 'sauce' in Náhuatl, the language of the Aztecs, but it is typically used to describe a very specific 'salsa', which is hot with chillies and flavoured with chocolate. It may sound like a strange combination, but the chocolate, although it cannot actually be tasted, adds a sultriness, a hint of exoticism to the overall dish which is impossible to describe. Ancho chillies are available in some supermarkets or from Cool Chile Company and chillipepperpete.com (page 17).

Ingredients

15g dried ancho chillies (see above)
500g tomatoes, halved
6 garlic cloves, unpeeled
2 tbsp olive oil
250g onions, peeled and coarsely chopped
400g red peppers, sliced into pieces about 2cm square
1 heaped tsp cumin seeds, toasted and medium ground (page 86)
1 tsp ground cinnamon
2 bay leaves
2 tbsp tahini paste (page 109)
15g dark chocolate (70% minimum cocoa solids), coarsely chopped
275g tinned or frozen sweetcorn, defrosted and well drained
15g toasted slivered almonds
Sea salt and freshly ground black pepper
Boiled rice or warm tortillas, to serve

Tip: The mole can be made in different stages over several days if it is easier: the tomato and chilli purée can be prepared and refrigerated, as can the onion and pepper mixture. It can then all be put together shortly before you are ready to eat. If anything, the mole, like any stew, improves with keeping.

Method

1   Heat a heavy frying pan over medium heat and toast the chillies, pressing down on them with a spatula, until they start to smell aromatic, about 3 minutes. Flip them over and do the same on the other side.

2   Place in a bowl, cover with boiling water, put a small saucepan lid or plate on top to keep them submerged, and set aside to soak for 30 minutes. Drain, discard the stems, seeds and ribs, and place in a food processor with 120ml of water.

3   While the chillies are soaking, preheat the grill to high. Line the grill pan with foil and arrange the tomatoes, cut side up, and garlic cloves on it. Grill 10cm from the heat for about 20 minutes, until lightly charred, turning the garlic cloves over halfway through.

4   Cool, then peel the garlic cloves and add them to the chillies in the food processor, along with the tomatoes and any juices. Process to a chunky purée.

5   Heat the olive oil in a frying pan and cook the onions and red pepper until soft and starting to brown. Add the spices and stir-fry for a couple of minutes before stirring in the bay leaves, chilli and tomato purée and some seasoning.

6   Cook the mole over medium heat for about 15 minutes, stirring often, until nice and thick. Add the tahini and chocolate, and cook for five minutes longer, until they have melted into the sauce. Stir in the sweetcorn and heat until steaming.

7   Check the seasoning and sprinkle with almonds.

8   Serve immediately with rice or tortillas.

Gâteau Piment with Guacamole

Makes 6 gâteaux

Many years ago, long before I started to cook professionally, I attended a series of Saturday cookery demonstrations at the Commonwealth Institute in London. They were organised by Meera Taneja, a highly gifted food writer and author of Indian Regional Cookery, which gave me my first taste of real Indian food – and the lunches, supplied by an Indian restaurant, were quite wonderful, spicy, mellow, utterly exotic compared to my normal, everyday diet. As I was a new vegetarian at the time, the vegetable dishes in particular were a real revelation, and when cooks from other Commonwealth countries demonstrated their favourite national dishes on successive Saturdays, I had the opportunity to glory in vegetarian food from around the globe: the flavours, textures and spices opened up a whole new world for me, and soya mince was banned from my kitchen forever. Gâteau piment from Mauritius has been a great favourite ever since.

Tip: Gâteau piment is a breakfast dish, served with French bread in Mauritius. I have replaced the baguette with wholemeal hamburger buns, as I prefer their texture against the crisp coating of the gâteau, and given it a Mexican twist with guacamole as an accompaniment to provide some richness and moisture.

Ingredients

250g red lentils, soaked overnight, rinsed and very well drained
150g red onions, finely chopped
1 large hottish red chilli, deseeded and finely chopped
2 garlic cloves, peeled and crushed
10g cumin seeds, toasted and coarsely ground (page 86)
2 tsp sea salt
50g red onions, coarsely chopped
1 garlic clove, peeled
3 tbsp olive oil and extra for frying
2 large ripe avocadoes
10g chives, coarsely snipped with scissors
1 large lime, juiced
6 wholemeal hamburger buns, split
Sliced tomatoes
Freshly ground black pepper

Method

1 For the gâteaux, place the first six ingredients in a food processor and grind quite finely. Shape the mixture into 6 patties – a pastry ring is very useful here! – and place them on a plate in the refrigerator for 30 minutes to firm up.

2 Rinse out the food processor, add the 50g of red onions, the whole garlic, 3 tbsp of olive oil, avocadoes, chives, 1 tbsp of lime juice and some seasoning. Process until fairly smooth and taste for acidity, adding more lime juice if it is not sharp enough. Check the seasoning and set the guacamole aside while you cook the gâteaux.

3 Heat some olive oil in a non-stick frying pan and add the gâteaux in a single layer – you may need to do this in two batches. Cook them on medium heat for about four minutes on each side, until they are crusty and lightly browned. Keep warm in the oven if necessary.

4 Place the gâteaux in the buns and top with a couple of slices of tomato and some guacamole.

5 Serve immediately.

Wild Mushroom Tacos

Makes 8 tacos

The flavour of wild mushrooms is earthy and woodsy but decidedly delicate and easily overpowered. Nevertheless, some partners do bring out their magic, and chilli is one of them. It needs to be a hint rather than an all out attack, and this Mexican recipe traditionally uses poblano chillies, which are mild and faintly fruity. They are not however widely available so I have replaced them with sweet red peppers and a dash of smoky chipotle chilli.

Ingredients

25g dried porcini mushrooms (see tip)
300g red peppers, grilled
3 tbsp olive oil and extra for frying
225g onions, peeled and sliced
2 garlic cloves, peeled and crushed
300g wild mushrooms, thoroughly cleaned
1 tsp bouillon powder
1 tsp dried Mexican or Greek oregano
1/2 tsp chipotle chilli powder or paste (page 29)
1 x quantity Roasted Tomato Sauce (page 24)
8 corn tortillas (page 146)
Cocktail sticks
5g fresh coriander, coarsely chopped
1 mild green chilli, deseeded and finely sliced
Sea salt and freshly ground black pepper

Method

1   Place the porcini in a small bowl and cover with boiling water. Leave to rehydrate for 30 minutes.

2   Skin the red peppers and cut the flesh into 1cm wide strips.

3   Heat 3 tbsp of olive oil in a large frying pan and cook the onions and garlic until soft and golden. Add the mushrooms, bouillon, oregano and chipotle, and stir-fry over medium heat until most of the moisture has evaporated.

Tip: Porcini mushrooms are widely available and have a wonderfully deep, woodsy flavour. They are expensive, but a little goes a long way and adding just two or three slices to fresh wild or even ordinary white or brown mushrooms makes a huge difference. They need to be reconstituted in hot water before use.

4 Scoop the porcini out of their soaking liquid with a slotted spoon and add to the pan. Carefully strain the liquid, leaving the last bit behind as it will be full of grit, and pour the strained liquid on top of the mushrooms. Season and cook, stirring often, until the mixture is quite dry. Stir in the grilled peppers and check the seasoning.

5 Heat the roasted tomato sauce.

6 Lay the tortillas out on the work surface and divide the mushroom mixture between them. Roll up tightly and secure with a cocktail stick.

7 Heat enough oil in a non-stick drying pan to just cover the bottom and cook the tacos, turning them as necessary, until they are golden all over. Transfer to warm plates and spoon over the tomato sauce.

8 Sprinkle with coriander and chillies and serve immediately.

Orange and Ginger Noodles

Serves 4

Tip:
Japanese
noodles like
soba and
udon are
available in
most large
supermarkets.
Clearspring
is a good,
organic
brand with
several
varieties,
such as
buckwheat
and brown
rice, which
are a
welcome
change from
all-wheat
Italian-style
pastas.

This is a gutsy combination of far Eastern ingredients and flavours like sesame oil and ginger, with a good kick from the chilli. It is quick and easy to make, as the sauce can be put together in pretty much the time it takes for the water to boil and the noodles to reach the right silky texture – although I must admit you do need to slice fairly fast! Soba or udon noodles are perfect for this dish, as their nutty richness works well with the other ingredients, but any kind of noodle can be used.

Ingredients

100ml toasted sesame oil
225g onions, peeled and sliced
2 garlic cloves, peeled and sliced
1 hottish red chilli (or more if you prefer!), deseeded and sliced
25g fresh ginger, peeled and cut into thin strips
3 tbsp tamari or shoyu soy sauce (page 52)
125ml ginger wine
1 large orange, juiced and 3 large oranges, segmented, juice reserved
1 tbsp cornflour
2 tbsp dark tahini (see tip on page 109)
1 tsp agave nectar or runny honey or to taste (page 24)
250g noodles
6 spring onions, trimmed and thinly sliced
10g coriander leaves, coarsely chopped
100g dry-roast peanuts
Sea salt and freshly ground black pepper

Method

1 Put a large pan of salted water on to boil for the noodles.

2 Heat the sesame oil in a large frying pan or wok, and stir in the onions, garlic, chilli and ginger. Cook over medium heat, stirring occasionally, until wilted and just starting to brown.

3 Mix the soy sauce, ginger wine, orange juice (including any from the segments) and cornflour in a cup and pour it into the pan. Stir and cook until it thickens. Whisk in the tahini and agave nectar.

need2know

4   Add the orange segments to the pan and set aside.

5   Cook the noodles according to the manufacturer's instructions and drain well.

6   Stir the noodles into the sauce and season with pepper and a sprinkling of salt – you don't need much as soy sauce is salty.

7   Add the spring onions, coriander and peanuts and check the seasoning and sweet/sour balance, stirring in a bit more agave or honey if necessary.

8   Divide the noodles between four warm bowls and serve immediately.

Chilli Bean and Potato Turnovers

Makes 12 turnovers

Filo pastry is light, crisp and fatless, making it a good choice on a vegan diet, as ready-made pastries like puff and shortcrust often contain butter or hydrogenated vegetable fats, while homemade pastry is time-consuming. Commercial filo on the other hand is excellent and just needs a lick of olive oil to give it a wonderfully crunchy texture.

Tip: Filo pastry dries out very quickly as it is incredibly thin, so it needs to be covered with a damp dishcloth once it is unwrapped, and individual sheets brushed with oil as soon as they are laid out.

Ingredients

2 tbsp olive oil and extra for brushing
375g potatoes, peeled, diced and steamed until tender
175g onions, peeled and coarsely chopped
2 garlic cloves, peeled and crushed
1 hottish red or green chilli, deseeded and finely sliced
2 tbsp sun-dried tomato purée
1 tbsp cumin seeds, toasted and medium ground (page 86)
1 x 400g tin black beans, drained and rinsed
8 sheets filo pastry (about 200g), measuring roughly 29cm x 35cm
Sea salt and freshly ground black pepper

Method

1   Heat the oil in a large non-stick frying pan, add the potatoes and sauté gently, stirring regularly, until golden. Remove to a plate with a slotted spoon.

2   Add the onions, garlic, chilli and some seasoning to the pan and stir-fry over medium heat until the onions are wilted and just starting to brown. Stir in the purée, cumin and black beans, and mash coarsely with the back of a wooden spoon, just enough to make the mixture hold together. Gently fold in the potatoes and check the seasoning.

3   Lay four sheets of filo pastry out on the work surface and brush them with oil. Top with the other four sheets and brush again with oil. Cut each double sheet into 3 equal long strips.

4   Divide the filling between the 12 strips, placing it at the end nearest you. Fold the left hand corner of the pastry up and over the filling to form a triangle. Fold the triangle up and to the right and so on up the strip until you have a neat triangular package. Brush the finished turnovers with oil and place them on a baking tray. The turnovers can be prepared up to this point several hours ahead and refrigerated.

5   Preheat the oven to 200°C/400°F/Gas Mark 6/fan oven 180°C and bake the turnovers for about 30 minutes, until golden and crisp.

6   Serve immediately.

Spiced Potato Wedges with Smoky Chilli Dip

Serves 4

The lightly crushed spices create a thin crust on the potatoes, giving them an aromatic crunch and burst of heat. If chilli is not your thing, you can leave out the chipotle and replace the Thai red curry paste with a mild curry paste – not quite the same but very delicious.

Ingredients

1 kg smallish potatoes, cut into wedges
1 tbsp whole cumin seeds, coarsely ground
1 tbsp whole coriander seeds, coarsely ground
1 tsp ground cinnamon
1/2 tsp Herbes de Provence or dried mixed herbs (see tip)
2 tbsp olive oil
1 tsp Thai red curry paste
1 tsp tamarind paste (see tip on page 150)
1 x quantity nut cheese made with cashews (page 87)
1 tsp chipotle chilli powder or to taste (page 29)
Sea salt and freshly ground black pepper

Method

1   Preheat the oven to 200°C/400°F/Gas Mark 6/fan oven 180°C. Place the potatoes in a roasting tin and toss with the spices, herbs, olive oil and seasoning. Cook, stirring occasionally, until golden and crusty, about 50 minutes.

2   Stir the curry and tamarind pastes into the cheese and check the seasoning.

3   Pile the potatoes into a warm serving dish and sprinkle with chipotle powder.

4   Serve immediately with the chilli dip.

Tip: Herbes de Provence is a mixture of dried, pungent herbs very typical of the cuisine of southern France. The composition can vary but it usually includes thyme, rosemary, summer savory, lavender, marjoram, sage, basil and oregano. It is wonderfully aromatic and lasts well in a sealed jar.

New World Vegetable Hotpot

Serves 4

Although I am calling this dish 'New World', I actually came across it for the first time on the island of La Gomera in the Canaries. This vegetable stew was served with 'goffio', a very solid and indigestible wheat porridge which sat in my tum like a lump of lead for the rest of the day, but the vegetables were sparky and delicious. I was struck by the fact that, other than the onions, they all originated in the New World and had obviously reached the islands several centuries before, courtesy of a Spanish galleon. The spices and sultanas on the other hand speak of the islands' proximity to Africa. I have added some Mexican chipotle chilli paste and topped it off with the welcome sharpness of yoghurt to cut the sweetness of the vegetables, making it all decidedly more Latin American than Canarian.

Tip: While tinned sweetcorn often has added sugar which makes it rather bland, the frozen version can be a bit chewy and requires slightly longer cooking.

Ingredients

1 kg tomatoes, halved

3 tbsp olive oil

500g sweet potato, peeled and cut into chunks

700g pumpkin or butternut squash, peeled, seeded and cut into chunks

1/4 tsp saffron threads

250ml vegetable stock, heated – water with bouillon powder will do

275g onions, peeled and chopped

4 garlic cloves, peeled and crushed

50g sultanas

1 tbsp coriander seeds, toasted and coarsely ground (page 86)

1 tbsp chipotle chilli paste (page 29)

275g tinned or frozen sweetcorn, rinsed and drained

25g slivered toasted almonds

10g flat leaf parsley, coarsely chopped

Plain soya yoghurt, well seasoned (page 52)

Sea salt and freshly ground black pepper

Method

1 Preheat the oven to 200°C/400°F/Gas Mark 6/fan oven 180°C. Arrange the tomatoes on a foil-lined roasting tin and season generously. Place on the top shelf of the oven and cook until they start to shrivel and blacken around the edges, about 45 minutes.

2 Place the sweet potato and pumpkin in another roasting tin, drizzle with 2 tbsp of olive oil and season well. Roast on the middle shelf of the oven under the tomatoes for about one hour, turning them over occasionally with a spatula, until they are golden.

3 When the tomatoes are ready, transfer them to a food processor and process until fairly smooth.

4 Crumble the saffron into the hot stock and leave it to dissolve for a few minutes.

5 Heat the remaining olive oil in a large saucepan and add the onions and garlic. Cook over medium heat, stirring occasionally, until they are soft and golden.

6 Stir in the roasted tomato purée, sultanas, ground coriander, chipotle paste, saffron mixture and some seasoning. Turn the heat right down, cover the saucepan and simmer for 15 minutes.

7 Uncover the saucepan and stir in the roasted vegetables and sweetcorn. Bring back to the boil and check the seasoning.

8 Ladle into 2 warm bowls, sprinkle with slivered almonds and parsley and top with a good dollop of yoghurt.

9 Serve immediately.

Hibiscus Flower Sorbet

Serves 6

This gloriously coloured sorbet is made from the flowers, or more precisely, the calyxes, of the hibiscus sabdariffa, which is native to Asia. It is commonly used worldwide as a tea and herbal remedy with many medicinal properties, including a valuable reputation as a laxative, a diuretic, an astringent and a slimming aid among others. The flavour is both sweet and tart, slightly tannic, with a hint of ripe summer fruit, reminiscent of a soft young wine. Dried hibiscus flowers are available from most health shops and by mail order from Cool Chile Company (page 19).

Tip: If you do not have an ice cream machine, place the chilled sorbet mixture in a plastic container in the freezer and whisk up with an electric beater every 30 minutes until thick.

Ingredients

500ml water
30g dried hibiscus flowers (see above)
150g caster sugar
2 tbsp Crème de Cassis liqueur
Mint leaves, to garnish (optional)

Method

1 Place the water and the flowers in a medium saucepan, bring to a boil and lower the heat. Cover and simmer for 10 minutes.

2 Remove the pan from the heat and let the mixture steep, covered, until cool. Strain, pressing down on the flowers to extract all the flavour.

3 Add the sugar and cassis and stir until the sugar is dissolved. Refrigerate until cold.

4 Freeze in an ice cream machine according to the manufacturer's instructions.

5 Serve in scoops and garnish with mint leaves.

Apple and Plum Brown Betty

Serves 4

A homely name for a very homely pudding! The Brown Betty is a great British classic, born of the need to use up stale bread and flavoured with whatever fruit was to hand or in season – and named perhaps after the seventeenth century ceramic Brown Betty teapot which was surely to be found in every household.

Ingredients

250g eating apples, peeled, cored and thinly sliced
200g purple plums, stoned and cut into eighths
125g soft wholemeal bread
4 tbsp walnut or hazelnut oil
90g light soft brown sugar
1 tsp ground cinnamon
100g walnut pieces
50g Demerara sugar
Vegan cream or ice cream, to serve (optional)
1ltr oven-proof, china dish

Method

1 Spread the fruit over the bottom of the dish.

2 Whizz the bread, oil, sugar and cinnamon in a food processor until you have medium fine breadcrumbs. Add the walnuts and process again for just a few seconds, to break them down.

3 Distribute the crumbs over the fruit and sprinkle with Demerara sugar.

4 Bake in a preheated oven at 200°C/400°F/Gas Mark 6/fan oven 180°C for about 30 minutes, until the crumbs are crisp and golden and the juices bubbling around the edges of the dish.

5 Cool for 10 minutes before serving.

Tip: Many different types of fruit can be used for this pudding and while the combination of apples and plums is very autumnal, ripe apricots and cherries make a lovely summer alternative.

Help List

The following organisations and websites are excellent sources of information and help on veganism, nutritional and environmental issues, as well as online shopping, publications, eating out, recipes and vegan/vegetarian events.

Dr Joel Fuhrman
www.drfuhrman.com
The website of the founder of the Center for Nutritional Medicine in the US. And an author and television broadcaster.

Dr Neal Barnard
www.pcrm.org
Dr Barnard is a clinical researcher, author and health advocate who has been the principal investigator or co-investigator on several clinical trials investigating the effects of diet on health. Facebook @NealBarnardMD

Friends of the Earth
www.friendsoftheearth.uk

The Kind Life
www.thekindlife.com
A website set up by actress Alicia Silverstone, author of The Kind Diet.

The Vegan Diet and Lifestyle – A Complete Guide
www.bestveganguide.com

The Vegan Forum
www.veganforum.com

The Vegan Society
www.vegansociety.com
Donald Watson House, 21 Hylton Street, Hockley, BIRMINGHAM, B18 6HJ, UK
Tel: 0121 523 1730
The Vegan Society is an educational charity which promotes and supports the vegan lifestyle.

The Vegetarian and Vegan Foundation

www.vegetarian.org.uk

8 York Court, Wilder Street, Bristol BS2 8QH.

Tel: 0117 970 5190

A charity set up to monitor and explain the increasing amount of scientific research linking diet to health – providing accurate information on which to make informed choices.

Vegatopia

www.vegatopia.org

Vegatopia is dedicated to providing a comprehensive academic resource on all things vegan.

VIVA! Vegetarians International Voice for Animals

www.viva.org.uk

8 York Court, Wilder Street, Bristol BS2 8QH, UK

Tel: 0117 944 1000

Viva! is a vegetarian and vegan organisation which campaigns energetically to end the abuse of animals killed for food. It is motivated by passion and backed by science. The website includes an excellent section, The L-Plate Vegan, on becoming a vegan.

Book List

Some interesting, useful and enjoyable books:

Colour me Vegan
by Colleen Patrick-Goudreau, Fair Winds – a bright and breezy book, packed with colourful recipes aimed at increasing nutritional intake.

Diet for a Small Planet
by Frances Moore Lappé, Ballantine Books – published in 1971, this was one of the first books to draw attention to the weaknesses of the global food system. Its message is still clear and bright forty years on.

Erotic Poetry for Vegans and Vegetarians
by Julie Mullen, UCVBooks – no recipes but plenty of laughs!

The Kind Diet
by Alicia Silverstone, Rodale Press – a lengthy, well-researched and informative introduction, and recipes which focus strongly on macrobiotics.

The Moosewood Cookbook
by Mollie Katzen, Ten Speed Press – a charmingly illustrated vegetarian cookery book with plenty of vegan recipes. This was the first, and to my mind, best book produced by the Moosewood Collective.

Veganomicon
by Isa Chandra Moskowitz and Terry Hope Romero, Da Capo Press – an amusing read and collection of recipes from two famous American vegans.

Vegan Fire and Spice
by Robin Robertson, VH Press – recipes to spice up your life!

World Food Café
by Chris and Carolyn Caldicott, Frances Lincoln – sumptuous photography and unusual vegan and vegetarian recipes from the founders of the World Food Café in London's Covent Garden.

You Are What You Eat
by Dr Gillian McKeith, Penguin Michael Joseph – colourful and easy to use nutritional guide, with useful details on the nutritional value of different foods.